BASKETBALL'S

TEN GREATEST DEFENSES

BASKETBALL'S
TEN GREATEST DEFENSES

William A. Healey

Professor, Physical Education/Men
Northern Illinois University
DeKalb, Illinois

Joseph W. Hartley

Assistant Professor, Physical Education/Men
Northern Illinois University
DeKalb, Illinois

PARKER PUBLISHING CO., INC. / WEST NYACK, N.Y.

743911

© 1975 by

PARKER PUBLISHING COMPANY,
INC.

West Nyack, N.Y.

Library of Congress Cataloging in Publication Data

Healey, William A
    Basketball's ten greatest defenses.

    1. Basketball--Defense. I. Hartley, Joseph W.,
1913-   joint author. II. Title.
GV888.H42   796.32'32   74-18356
ISBN 0-13-069252-2

Printed in the United States of America

To the unheralded defensive players
in the game–the real scorers.

KEY TO ALL DIAGRAMS

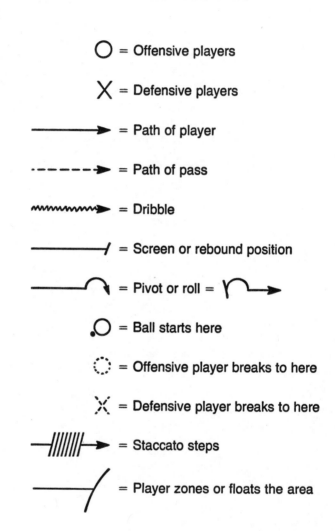

O = Offensive players

X = Defensive players

⟶ = Path of player

⤍ = Path of pass

∿∿∿⟶ = Dribble

⟶⫽ = Screen or rebound position

⟶⤸ = Pivot or roll = ⌐⟶

.O = Ball starts here

⦂⦂ = Offensive player breaks to here

X̶ = Defensive player breaks to here

⊣⫽⫽⫽⊢⟶ = Staccato steps

⟶⟋ = Player zones or floats the area

Acknowledgments

If the combined coaching years of the authors of this book were totaled, the resultant figure would make an impressive sounding number of years of coaching experiences. If, after this experience, we could not write a book or books about our chosen profession of coaching basketball, we would indeed feel inadequate. To be able to do so is a pleasurable experience, and an opportunity for which we are grateful. The resultant book is the outcome of many contacts, many experiences, much learning, many struggles, and the contribution of nameless numbers of contacts. Every contact, every experience in the lives of the authors was a contribution. To name all the contributors would be impossible, and to name some means someone has been left out, so acknowledgments by names will not be attempted. We feel indebted to all. Certainly our thoughts and our work in such a project as this is the result of everything that has become a part of us.

Perhaps to more than anyone else, gratitude should be expressed to the young men who played on our teams throughout our years of coaching. From them we have received far more than we could give. These players have gone into successful careers as coaches, teachers, doctors, businessmen, professional athletes, professional men, and one is an astronaut. As we look back over these men and what they have become, we cannot think of one who has been a failure. All have been highly successful. To have been a small part of their lives is greatly appreciated by the authors.

We also wish to make expressions of gratitude to our fellow coaches in the profession and to the men who coached us. Athletics and coaching are constant learning and teaching processes. We learned from all with whom we came in contact.

While we acknowledge that this book is the product of all, we sincerely hope that all who pick it up and read through its pages will benefit and profit from the experience.

Why This Book Is Important

Defense has never been the most popular word in basketball. Defensive play has never had the appeal for players, fans, or coaches that the offensive phase of the game has had. There are many reasons for this, the main one being that the players themselves like this part of the game better. They like to score and the fans like to see the ball go through the net. The sports writers popularize the scorer and consequently place a great deal of emphasis on scoring. They seldom mention the brillant play of the defensive player even though he may have been instrumental in winning the game. For example, the box score supposedly showing the detailed results of the game gives the offensive accomplishments of the players, not the defensive accomplishments.

PLAYER RECOGNITION FOR DEFENSIVE PLAY

Most players like to receive some recognition and it does not take them long to find that the best way to do this is to score points. Coaches, in attempting to obtain better defensive play from their players, have had to resort to the use of gimmicks of all kinds in their search for motivational techniques.

EARLY WRITINGS ON DEFENSIVE BASKETBALL

Early writings on the subject of basketball failed to stress defense, but placed a great deal of emphasis on offense and the offensive aspects of the game. It was a long time before a book appeared on the market that was devoted entirely to the techniques of defensive play. However, in the last few years there have been several such books that are devoted exclusively to defensive concepts and techniques. Some of these books have developed special systems such as pressure defenses, match-up-defenses, stunting defenses, and other special slides, glides, and switches. One of the earlier books on basketball devoted exclusively to defense was called, *Techniques and Tactics of Basketball Defense*, written by Blair Gullion of Washington University. This book appeared as late as 1951 and stressed the techniques and concepts of defensive play in great detail. It was a much-needed book and contributed a great deal to the game of basketball. There have been other such publications since then, but few as detailed as Gullion's book.

INFLUENCE OF RULES ON DEFENSIVE PLAY

The rules makers have encountered many problems in making rules to cope with the defensive tactics used by players, while at the same time being aware that the offensive part of the game was extremely popular. Offense, the popular spectator phase of the game, could not be hampered too much, and yet defensive effectiveness should not be destroyed. Therefore it can be readily seen that one of the greatest concerns of the rules makers was to keep the rules up-to-date so that a proper balance between offense and defense could be maintained and at the same time retain the fan and spectator appeal. These efforts have been fruitful, but have usually given a slight edge to the offense, enough to keep the spectator interest without penalizing the defense too severely. Today's high-scoring contests sometimes cause concern among the defensive advocates of the game as to just how much defensive play takes place during these games.

DEVELOPMENT OF DEFENSIVE PLAY

Defensive play and techniques have been developed and improved greatly throughout the history of the game. However, it has not kept pace with the advancement and rapid changes of the offensive concepts, techniques, and tactics. This has caused some concern, and it could be the result, to some extent at least, of the rules under which the game is played. The explosive nature of the offensive development of the game appears to have caused the lag in the defensive improvement. The rules makers probably have been guilty to some degree, at least, in giving the edge to the offensive phase of the game so that it would not lose its spectator appeal. However, even though the defensive phases of the game have lagged behind compared to the offense, defensive play has improved greatly.

PURPOSE OF THE BOOK

It is the intent of the authors of this book to present the basic fundamentals of defensive play necessary to establish a sound defensive game.

The basic concepts of defensive play for the individual as well as team play will be presented. These concepts are the foundation fundamentals necessary to establish sound and effective play using any type of defense. Following the development of the basic concepts of defensive play, ten different applications of the basic concepts will be presented as ten different defenses. Actually, the defenses presented will be a different application of the same fundamentals or concepts. Each application will be a different defense. Also, in order to not be limited to the number "ten," some optional defenses will also be presented. These defenses can be integrated into the system or added to it. Variations in player personnel from year to year and variations in opponents' play, style, and personnel will often require additions to, deletions from, or substitutions for some of the basic applications of the defenses presented. This is the reason for presenting the optional defenses.

The defensive concepts and fundamentals along with the different applications constitute a defensive system that has been successfully employed and used by many coaches. The idea of a team effectively using and applying "ten" different defenses seems at first to be an impossible assignment. However, when it is realized that the concepts are all the same with a few variations, it is not as difficult a task as it first appears to be. With good effective motivation, the task can be accomplished and the team will acquire better offensive and defensive balance.

ABILITY OF PLAYERS TO MASTER DEFENSIVE CONCEPTS

Not all teams will be able to master the complete set of ten defenses, although this is not outside the realm of possibility. Deletions from and additions to the defensive applications can be made according to the progress the team makes and the ability of the players to assimilate the necessary information.

VALUES DERIVED FROM THIS BOOK

Coaches, players, and others who read this book will learn about the fundamental concepts necessary to play effective defense. In addition they will learn how to apply ten different defenses, along with the option possibilities, and how to teach them.

Such defensive play should add trophies to the championship trophy case and at the same time develop good teams and outstanding young men. Selling the players on playing good rough, rugged, aggressive defense has always been a challenge to every coach. Getting the players to think, like, live, and then play defense is the answer. One of the best selling points in this respect is via the defensive route. To play defense as it should be played and as it is explained in the pages of this book is to destroy the offensive play of the opponents, and to cut down on the amount of time that they have possession of the ball. This will add to the time your team has possession of the ball and as a result will enhance your opportunities to score. Expert defensive play gives the team more offensive power and more scoring punch. It returns the ball to you by forcing the opponents to make mistakes.

The team that can effectively apply these defensive concepts and use the different applications as described will win games and championships.

If you want to score, play defense.

Bill Healey
Joe Hartley

Contents

Point of contact—just back of the ten-second division line. Reasons for using the defense. The principle of the 20 overshift. Forcing the offense to the outside. Rule changes that favor the 20 defense. The mid-court area rule and how it should be used in the 20 defense. Responsibilities of the various positions in the defense. Possible trap areas that can be applied with the defense. The 20 defense as the beginning of the pressure defense series.

Point of contact. Use of the "20 principle" in the overshift. Application of the 10 principle possible. Two-timing possibilities and trap areas to exploit. Responsibility of each position in the defense. Weak-side play and responsibility. Pressure points and aim of the defense. Trap dilemmas. Help and switching situations to bring pressure on the ball. Zonish principles applied.

Full-court man-to-man press. Points of contact, and variations in points of attack. Basic pressing ideas to teach. A harassing defense. Mental and physical requirements of players needed to play the defense. First duty of the defense to stop the dribbler. Pressuring the thrower-in. Double-teaming the inbounds pass. Two ways to apply the defense—assigned opponent and pick up the nearest opponent. How to compensate for mistakes. Help or switch situations. Fundamental ideas to constantly stress. Reasons for using the full-court press. Avoiding screens and picks from the rear. Applying both the 10 and 20 principles of the overshift in the 40 defense.

Applied to the 10 defensive area. A 1-2-2 zone defense. Zone principles. How and when applied or used. Advantages. Disad-

6   THE NUMBER 11 DEFENSE, *cont.*

vantages. Mannish features. Advantages of changes from 10 to
11.

A 2-3 zone defense. Zone features and areas. Applied to the 10
defensive area. Zone principles. How and when used. Advantages and disadvantages. Making it mannish. Changing from 10 to
12, or from 11 to 12.

A 1-3-1 zone defense. Zone features and areas of coverage for
each player. Shifting so as to keep three defensive men between
the ball and the basket. The shifts and the two-timing features.
Strengths and weaknesses. When to use. Change-of-pace features. When to apply. Changing from a 10 to a 13 or from an 11 or
12 to a 13 defense. Applied in the 10 defensive area.

A special trap defense applied in the 30 defensive area. Features
of the trap and how applied. Zone principles applied. Man-to-man
principles used. Using the trap areas and coffin corners. Advantages of the back-court trap. Present rule favoring the trap in the
mid-court area. Guarding the nearest pass receivers. The long
pass possibilities to the free man. How to combat and prevent.

A three-fourths to a half-court zone press applied in the 30 defensive area. A 1-2-2 alignment. Responsibilities of players in various
assignments. Zone principles applied. Press situations used.
Mannish features employed. Appropriate times to apply the defense. Trap possibilities and shifts to cover possible outlet passes.

An all-court zone press—applied to the 40 area. Zone principles.

11   THE NUMBER 41 DEFENSE, *cont.*

Mannish features. Coverage areas for each player. Forcing passes. Two-timing situations. Going for the interceptions. The second pass. Protecting against the cheap basket. Variations in the front line personnel. The Big 41 and the normal 41. When to apply the defense to advantage. The double shift. When and how to release pressure.

12   THE NUMBER 10T, 14, AND 15 DEFENSES: Combination Defenses 167

10T defense—an option to the 10 defense. More team application with more emphasis on the ball. Assignments and alignments. Principles of the defense. Switching and sliding. Zonish and mannish features. Team features and how to apply.
14 defense—a special situation defense—a box zone with a one man-to-man or a diamond zone with one man-to-man.
15 defense—a scramble defense—three men zoning and two men playing man-to-man—or a two-man zone and three men playing man-to-man. Used strictly for scramble purposes.

13   THE NUMBER 42, 43, AND 44 DEFENSES: Variations of the Zone Press..185

42 defense—a 2-1-2 full-court zone press. Assignments, shifts, and how it works.
43 defense—a 3-2 zone press—applied to the 40 area. Assignments, shifts, how it works, and application of pressure.
44 defense—a 2-2-1 zone press applied to the 40 area. Player assignments, application of pressure, pressure areas, forcing passes, two-timing situations, going for interceptions, protecting against the cheap basket, and application in play.

14   CYCLING OR ROTATING THE DEFENSES 195

Purpose of cycling the defenses. Rotation or cycling by numbers.

14 CYCLING OR ROTATING THE DEFENSES, *cont.*

Rotation by quarters. Running partial cycles. Changing the defenses. Defensive captains and uses. Changing the cycles. Partial cycles. Keeping the opposition offense constantly upset and unable to do the thing they want to do. The man-to-man cycle—10, 20, 30, and 40. The press cycle—10, 20, 30, 31Z, 40, and 41. Area cycles—10, 11, 12, 13, 14, plus options. 10 and 20 cycles, 30 cycles, and 40 cycles. Running zone cycles. Zone press cycles.

Developing the defensive attitude. Selling the defensive philosophy. Giving recognition of defensive play and performance. Developing community awareness of defensive play. What defensive coaching will do for the team. Coaching offense via the defensive method, and coaching defense via the offensive method.

1

Defensive Concepts for Individual Play

Successful defensive play in basketball is based on sound fundamentals. A defensive system that contributes to the success of the team must be founded upon basic concepts and ideas that are fundamentally sound. This chapter will present these fundamental concepts and describe the necessary movements that must be mastered by every member of the team if this success is to be forthcoming. There are basic concepts that must be learned by every individual player. There are also basic concepts that must be mastered by the team as a unit. Each team member has two areas of responsibility that he must master. First, he must know and be able to perform the needed basic individual defensive skills; and second, he must know and be able to perform the basic team concepts that are necessary to make the defense function as a complete team effort. The latter concept is necessary and important if the defense is to be successful. Although defensive play is based on the individual performance of players using these basic fundamental concepts, the individual moves of all the players must be finely tuned and coordinated into a total team effort. This in turn will result in the five players functioning as a well-synchronized unit.

TEACHING INDIVIDUAL FUNDAMENTALS

The teaching of defense must begin with the individual player, and it must be done on an individual basis. If the individual players are well-grounded in the fundamentals of defensive play, the coach can mold together a good team defense easily and quickly. Coaches usually spend much more time teaching players what to do when they have the ball, or what to do when they get the ball. This can hardly be justified when the probable ball-control time possibilities of each player in a game is limited.

Take two teams, for instance, that are of equal ability. It could be assumed that because both have equal ability, each team would control the ball 50% of the time. A high school game is 32 minutes in length. Divide 32 by 2—and the possible ball control time for one team is 16 minutes. The 16 minutes of possession time could be shared by 5 players on the team. Unless the team has a "ball-hog" on the team, it could be assumed that ball possession time could be equally shared by the players. Divide 16 minutes by 5. This gives a time of 3.2 minutes (3 minutes and 12 seconds) that a player will, on the average, be playing the game with the ball in his actual possession. This is about 10% of the entire game time. In a college game of 40 minutes, the possession time, based on the above formula, would be 4 minutes of actual playing time. This would figure to be the same percentage of time that each player has possession of the ball. What about the other 90% of the game time that the player will be playing in the game without having possession of the ball? Shouldn't he be taught how to play during this 90% of the game, 50% of which will largely be spent on defense? In view of the above philosophical reasoning and thinking, certainly many coaches have not, and do not spend nearly enough time teaching the players what to do or how to perform on offense without the ball, or how to effectively play defense against the opponent when they have the ball.

The coach must sell the idea to the players that they must be whole players—that to be really good players, they must play both an effective game while on offense without the ball, and also while on defense. If the players can be convinced that by effective defensive play they can decrease the ball-control time of the opponent, and as a result increase their own ball-control time, the coach is on his way to selling the players on the idea that good defensive play can win games. The players must be convinced that good defensive play will help them win games, if they have a reasonably good offense.

THE STANCE

The question of teaching defense may be, "Where to begin?" One coach was heard to say, "you begin with the *stance*, and you end with the *stance*." This is a good statement and well put.

The *stance*, as explained in this book, refers to the position of the feet and the body of the defensive player while guarding an offensive player. It could be further defined as the best arrangement of body parts to enable the defensive player to attack or counter the opponents' offensive moves. Proper stance is an important requisite of individual defensive play. Defensive action demands that all players possess the ability to move in any direction quickly and easily. Stability, balance, and the ability to move quickly are all factors that must be taken into consideration when teaching a stance. The stance while guarding a man with the ball and guarding a man without the ball will differ somewhat, and will be explained.

Since the man with the ball is always the focal point of the defense, then it is obvious that teaching defense should begin with the stance a defensive player should have when guarding a man with the ball. *Begin with the feet*. Take a boxer's stance (sometimes called a fencer's stance) with one foot definitely in front of the other in a comfortable position. The feet should be comfortably and naturally spread, about shoulder width apart. Comfort is important, and the feet should not be spread either too wide, or be too close together. A stance that is either too wide or too narrow can vitally affect the player's stability, balance, and ability to move quickly. Either foot may be advanced, but an important factor to be considered is which way the guard may want to force the offensive player in a given situation. The defensive player should have as his forward foot the one opposite to the direction in which he desires to drive the offensive player. This will be discussed further in the "Principle of the Overshift." The distance that one foot is advanced in front of the other will vary or differ with each player. Usually the toe of the back foot will be about even with the heel of the front foot. It is important that the player has a natural "feel" in his stance.

The heel of the back foot or the entire sole of the shoe of the back foot *must be on the floor*. The weight of the body should be distributed evenly over both feet. The weight should be concentrated on the full soles of the shoes. However, if a situation exists where the weight of the body is concentrated more on one foot than the other, one should favor the back foot. The center of gravity for the entire body should never fall outside the base of the stance. It should always be maintained between the feet, and be inside the base.

The defensive player should point the toe of the front foot right at, or in the direction of, the opponent and use the boxer's stance. The back foot should point at a 40° to 90° angle away from the opponent. The back foot should be planted firmly on the floor.

Going up from the feet—the defensive player should bend or flex the knees, drop the hips, and keep the trunk erect (somewhat coiled) with the hips and buttocks (tail) low. The hands should be kept low and be coordinated with the movements of the feet. All players should be coached to keep the hands low when guarding the dribbler. When guarding the passer, the hands should be played so as to prevent passes in the area around the head and shoulders. When guarding the shooter, one hand should be extended straight up so the opponent is forced to shoot over it.

Analyzing the *stance* still further, it can be seen that the boxer's stance, the use of which is advocated, stresses player stability and balance. It gives the player mobility and quick maneuverability in all directions. The boxer's stance gives the body more stability in moving from front to rear as well as laterally. If for some reason it is necessary to have the weight concentrated on one foot more than the other, it should favor the back foot. This enables the defensive player to make his move either backward or forward. It enables the player to make a quick forward thrust with the attack step, and still be ready to execute a *retreat step*. Insistence that the defensive player should never use his hands except in coordination with the movements of his feet prevents the player from making forward lunges. This results in the shifting of his weight and center of gravity so far forward that a *retreat step* cannot be made, or if made, it can be done only after the opponent has dribbled past the defensive player. This can happen because of his having shifted the center of gravity outside the base of his body forward, or at least toward the front edge of the base. Advocate that against a shooter, the defensive player should extend one hand straight up in the air to prevent the shifting of the center of gravity of the body too far forward. This extended hand also means that the shooter will have to be farther back from the basket to clear the guard's hand. This decreases the chances of making the shot good.

An important point to stress in teaching defense to any player is—*do not play defense with your hands. You play defense with your mind and your feet*. Other important points that should be stressed are: The feet must move before or simultaneously with the hands, since the hands tend to commit the player too much. The hands and feet should move together. If the player moves his feet first, or his hands move with his feet or after the foot movements are made, then the hand movements are acceptable. If the player will conform to these principles, he will not make too much commitment with the hands and as a result will not allow himself to be thrown forward to such an extent that his center of gravity will be thrown outside the defensive base. Such a commitment would make the player vulnerable to a drive and as a result allow the offensive player to outmaneuver him. If the player does not make these hand commitments, which in turn throw the center of gravity of the body weight beyond the defensive base, or outside the feet, the player will be able to move quickly in any direction and be able to stay with the player he is guarding. The defensive player must be in a position to move backward and prevent the offensive player from moving around him. This does not mean, however, that the hands are not to be used in defensive play. In fact, the direct opposite is true. However, the hand commitments should never exceed the movements as previously described. After a player learns to make his defensive movements properly, coordinating both his mind and his feet, then hand movements should be encouraged. They can be used very effectively to harass, to distract, and to bother the opponent. The defensive player should be encouraged to make these hand movements from underneath when guarding the ball handler. This should be done in conjunction with the foot movements. Different hand movements should be used to guard a shooter, a passer, a dribbler, and a cutter.

THE FIRST MOVE—THE RETREAT STEP

Beginning with the *stance* position just described—which has the defensive player guarding an offensive player with the ball—regardless of the move of the opponent, the first move of the defensive player is always back in what is called a *retreat step*. To be in a guarding position against an opponent with the ball, the defensive player should be close enough to reach out and touch him. To be farther away, the guard would not be close enough to attack or counter his moves. The retreat step is a spring or bounce to the rear type of movement, and not a series of steps. In executing this step, the hips must be dropped low, the knees must be bent, and the arms must be used to obtain the necessary lift. The position of the feet remains the same as at the start of the step. If after making the retreat step, the offensive player drives, the defensive player must make whatever adjustment is necessary and move with him in a lateral glide. If the offensive player has only executed a fake movement, the defensive player will do a reverse of the retreat step. He does this by bouncing forward using the attack step, thereby placing himself again in an excellent position to harass the ball handler.

These stance positions and movements just described, along with the first move, are all in conformity with the principles of body mechanics and the laws of physics which give stability and balance. They will contribute to quick movements by the player, all of which will give him optimum possibilities for countering and attacking the offensive player.

THE PRINCIPLE OF THE OVERSHIFT

The next phase of the individual defensive teaching process concerns the *principle of the overshift* in the stance, as it affects the direction in which the defensive player may want to force the offensive player. Ordinarily, the defensive player would be told when he takes his *stance* that personal comfort could decide which foot is forward, but another very important factor to be considered in determining which foot is forward is in what direction the defensive player may want to force the offensive player, in a given situation. The defensive player should have as his forward foot, the foot opposite to the direction in which he desires to force the offensive player in his move. For example, if the defensive player wants to force the offensive player to the left, he would take a defensive stance with the right foot forward, and the left foot back. He would overshift the offensive player to his (defensive) own right as much as one-half his width or more. He would place his left shoulder about even with the midsection of the opponent. If the offensive player drives strongly to his own left, the overshift could be as much as one whole body-width. In an overshift this strong, the defensive player might place his own left shoulder about even with, or directly opposite to the opponent's left shoulder. In using the overshift, one thing is certain—the defensive player must always be ready to move with the offensive player in a guarding position when he is forced to move in the desired direction. If the defensive player wishes to force the offensive player to move to the defensive player's right, he should take a stance with the left foot forward, and overshift to his left a distance one-half his body width. At the same time he should be certain he is ready to move with his opponent when he moves to his right. Also, he should always make sure that he is able to recover and move with the offensive player on a lateral glide, should his opponent execute a drive to the defensive player's right.

In using the overshift principle, regardless of the offensive player's move, or fake—the first move of the defensive player is always backward off the back foot in a *retreat step*. If the offensive player has moved in the opposite direction of the overshift, the defensive player, after executing the retreat step, makes whatever adjustment is necessary. He should move into a lateral, or an oblique lateral glide with the offensive player, always keeping his opponent to the outside. If he cannot keep up with him using this glide, he should break into a fighting run until he is able to obtain an advantageous position on him. He should then glide into the attacking position again. Making the first move properly is very important. If the first and second moves are properly made by the defensive player, the chances of the offensive player's being successful in driving around or past him are very slim indeed.

If the offensive player drives in the opposite direction of the overshift, or drives the front foot and leg of the defensive player, then the defensive player must adjust to this move. To make the proper adjustment requires one extra move. However, the added distance that the offensive player will have to move against the overshift will more than compensate for this extra movement. For example, if the defensive player is in an overshift to his left, with the left foot forward in an effort to drive the offensive player to the defensive right (assuming that the offensive player insists on driving to the defensive player's left), the first move of the defensive player would be as usual, backward off the back foot using a *retreat step*. Since the dribbler is driving toward the side of the forward foot and opposite the side of the open stance of the defensive player, the defensive player must reverse his foot position so that his stance will be open to the side of the path of the offensive player. This will enable him to move into the proper glide step action. This can be accomplished in the following manner:

Immediately after the action just described, as soon as the retreat step is completed, the defensive player should move his left arm and shoulder backward in a definite tug to the rear, taking along the entire left side of his body. This will place the left foot and leg to the rear so that his stance will be open and facing the path that will be taken by the offensive player. This is often referred to as a *drop step*. He will now be in a position that will enable him to go into the proper glide that he should use in guarding the dribbler.

Diagram 1-1 shows a mechanical analysis of this movement. The chart, representing two players, shows how the overshift principle forces the offensive player to transverse a greater distance than the defensive player who is guarding him. This gives the advantage to the defensive player if the retreat step and the drop step movements are executed correctly.

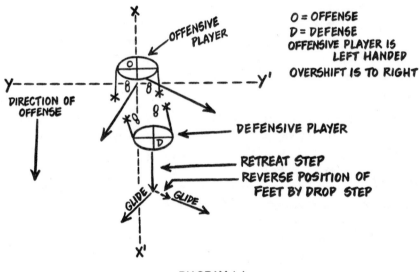

DIAGRAM 1-1

To circumvent the defensive player, using his favorite movement (assuming that this offensive player is left handed and that his strong move is to his left) the offensive player must make his cut on a larger angle, and as a result he must travel a greater distance. This tends to discourage the offensive player from making such a move. However, if he insists on making the move, the defensive player can fully compensate by making a countermove that involves one extra movement.

After his retreat step, he reverses the position of his feet (by making the drop step move previously described) and is then ready to move into the lateral glide he should use in guarding the offensive player. The extra foot movement used by the defensive player is not nearly as much of a handicap to him as is the added distance and angle of movement imposed upon the offensive player. This maneuver usually enables the defensive player to counter the offensive player's movement, and as a result offset any advantage he may have. If the offensive player elects to go around the defensive player using his weaker move (in this instance to his own right), the offensive player has less distance to travel. However, this move is more easily countered by the defensive player due to the fact that the movement is toward the side of the open stance, and the defensive player is ready to move with him in a lateral glide, after a retreat step.

THE GLIDE STEP

The glide or the steps used in executing the glide are fundamental for the footwork used in movements in guarding the offensive player. The glide is also used for establishing the path of the defensive player which must be in proper relationship to the path of the dribbler, or the offensive player. The glide can be executed laterally to the right, left, or obliquely in either direction. In executing the glide, *both feet must move simultaneously* using a hopping movement. The distance between the feet may be slightly wider than is used in the original boxer's stance, but usually it is approximately the same. The feet in this movement will be even and parallel, with neither one advanced. The body should be coiled slightly, and the arms, shoulders, and hips must be used to gain the "lift" needed to execute the hopping movement. The feet should be comfortably spread. Too wide a spread interferes with the body lift needed in executing the hopping movement. The feet should be perpendicular to a line paralleling the path of the offensive player, and at a distance that would enable the defensive player to reach out and touch the offensive player. The soles of the shoes should be on the floor, but the defensive player should carry his weight in executing this glide on the balls of the feet. His weight should be evenly distributed on both feet. The feet should never be crossed while the player is executing the gliding motion. This is a fundamental principle of this maneuver. The knees should be flexed or bent, the hips should be dropped, and the body should be slightly coiled or in a crouched position. The arms should be carried forward and to the side. The height of the hands should depend on the defensive situation —being low on a dribbler, and near full extension if the threat of an underbasket shot is evidenced. The head should be erect, with the upper part of the body fairly straight in order to provide the balance necessary for position changes, or for a change in the defensive path to meet the various offensive moves.

In using the glide movement, when both feet are moved simultaneously, the player will have better stability and balance. He will be able to hold his position better and cannot be faked out of it easily. As an example let us assume that the player moved one foot at a time in the glide movement. If he is moving to the right, he would move the right foot and then the left. The player would tend to move the right foot about 8 to 12 inches, and then follow with a movement of the left foot in a much greater move. This would bring the two feet closer together in a much narrower stance, and it would affect two natural laws of physics—that of equilibrium and stability. Stability is directly proportional to the area of the base on which the body rests. If the feet are closer together, the area of the base is smaller, and as a result, the body has less stability and balance. For equilibrium to exist, the center of gravity of a body must fall within its base. For example, if the feet are brought together too closely in this type of gliding movement, then any fake movement by the offensive player which would necessitate a countermove by the defensive player when his feet are so situated, could easily change his center of gravity so that it would fall outside the base of the body. A countermove by the offensive player would leave the defensive player in a disadvantageous position while he was attempting to recover his balance. Also, when the defensive player moves first one foot and then the other in sequential movements rather than in simultaneous movements, when he brings his feet closer together in a narrower stance, he also tends to raise the height of the center of gravity of the body. This type of movement brings into play the principle that the stability of a body is indirectly proportional to the distance of the center of gravity of the body above the base. With this height increase in the center of gravity above the base, or stance, certainly this player will have less balance and stability and be more vulnerable to fakes and countermoves by the offense.

In advocating the fundamental principle that the feet should never be crossed when using the gliding motion, another very important natural law or principle of equilibrium is brought into focus. When the feet are crossed, not only is the stance narrowed, but there is a shifting of the weight of the body to such an extent that the center of gravity of the body would be thrown almost, if not completely, outside the base. For equilibrium to exist, the center of gravity of a body must fall within its base. Certainly when a defensive player crosses his feet and legs while using the gliding movement he can be reversed very quickly by the offensive player due to this improper shifting of the weight with respect to the base or stance that he has taken.

GUARDING THE DRIBBLER

In guarding the dribbler, the defensive player must know what the dribbler can do to beat him. Most of the time the dribbler will beat him in the direction in which the dribbler is going. The defensive player must get *ahead of the dribbler* regardless of the direction in which he is moving. It must be remembered that the dribbler may also slow up, change pace, put on a new burst of speed, jockey, bob, weave, or fake with his head and shoulders, or do a cross-over dribble. The hand that will protect on the cross-over dribble should be kept down. The other hand should be kept up. The stance should be open to the side of the dribbler. The defensive player should not go with the ball, or watch it. He should not be taken in by a change of pace, a slow-down movement followed by a burst-out, or by fakes. He should be prepared for these kinds of maneuvers and try to get the dribbler to pick up the ball and kill the dribble. When he does, attack him—flog him good. Make him move it. Harass him. The defensive man can now commit himself, since the dribbler has committed himself by stopping the dribble. The defensive player should now force his opponent either to get rid of the ball, be forced into a jump ball situation, or better still, throw the ball up for a steal. After the commitment of stopping the dribble has been made by the offensive player, the defensive player's teammates should play *hard* for interceptions.

GUARDING THE MAN WITHOUT THE BALL

When the player with the ball passes off to a teammate, the position of the defensive player must change immediately. His position will be determined by a number of factors. First considerations will be the defensive application being made at the time. This will determine the actions of the defensive player to a great extent. Generally speaking though, the defensive player will determine his play by the consideration of two imaginary lines—one drawn from the ball to the man he is guarding, and the other a line drawn from the same opponent to the basket. Immediately after the offensive player has passed the ball to a teammate, the defensive player drops off on the imaginary line from the opponent to the basket. He now changes his stance so that he can watch his offensive opponent and the ball. This drop-off or fall away is often referred to as a *sag*, or a *float*. In reality it is an application of a *zone* principle. The defensive man is playing both his man and the ball. His first move is a drop-off on the line toward the basket from his offensive opponent. He may later make adjustments from this line toward the second imaginary line from the ball to the opponent. The distance he drops off will be determined by a number of factors such as his speed, his opponent's speed, the distance the ball is from his opponent, and the speed with which the opponents move and pass the ball. Alertness and acuity must be developed in these situations. The defensive player should not lose his stance when he does this float or drop-off move. He should not change his center of gravity by standing up higher in a more relaxed position. He should remain low and in a balanced position, ready to play his opponent and to counter any of his moves. If and when his opponent moves into the vital scoring areas close to the basket, he should maneuver himself into a position that will prevent his opponent from receiving the ball while in these vital areas. Allowing the opponent to receive the ball in these areas is equivalent to giving the opponents two points. In this situation the imaginary line from the opponent to the ball comes into play and becomes more pertinent. In many of these situations the defensive player should play directly on this line, and directly in front of the opponent. In other situations, he will play with his front foot on this line, so as to prevent his offensive opponent from receiving the ball. This will vary in the different defensive applications and will be developed in breadth in later chapters of this book.

In defensing the player without the ball, the coach should work hard to teach his players peripheral vision on the weak side. (The weak side is the side away from the ball.) Every time the ball is dribbled or passed by the opponents, the defensive player must make constant adjustments in his position so that he will be able to see the ball, and at the same time keep his defensive position in relation to his opponent. He must play his man *through the ball*. He must be ingrained with the philosophy and thinking that no opponent shall ever be allowed to break from the weak side areas and receive the ball in the vital scoring areas. This will often necessitate having the defensive player play in *front* of the opponent and directly between him and the ball while facing the ball. At other times it will involve watching the player in the weak side area over his shoulders, or partially siding, or playing sideways to him, or siding him in such a manner as to keep him from receiving the ball. While the focal point of the defense is always on the player with the ball, it is also important in many situations to prevent a player from receiving the ball where he wants to receive it, and the defense must play accordingly.

GUARDING THE JUMP-SHOOTER

The jump-shot is the most phenomenal shot in the game today. It has completely revolutionized the offensive game. It is the most difficult of all shots to guard, if it is executed properly. The coach must put special emphasis on developing techniques for defensing this shot, and especially the jump-shooters that have deadly accuracy. Today, very few players shoot anything else but a jump-shot, so if the defense can prevent the drive, and prevent the jump-shooter from getting a good shot, the defense is bound to be successful. Defensing the jump-shot may at times require what would, in most situations, be regarded as unorthodox or unusual methods of prevention. What makes the jump-shot so difficult to defense is that to properly defense it, the defensive man must know when the player is going to shoot, and be able to jump with him, and go as high as he does—a very difficult feat, and almost impossible if the offensive player has good head and shoulder fakes. The following pointers or suggestions are offered as solutions to defensing the jump-shooter.

1. Prevent the real tough jump-shooter from getting the ball every time it can possibly be done.

2. If the jump-shooter does get the ball, chase him, and drive him from his most favorable shooting spots and to his least favored areas.
3. Play him so tight that he is forced to go around the defensive player. Move in on him—pressure him, especially with the hands moving in from underneath, and upward. Be sure when he goes around that he is going where help can be secured from a teammate—then gang him.
4. At times, when the jump-shooter raises the ball to a shooting position, or to a position head high or above—jump in as close as possible to him with a wide square stance and harass him. This may be somewhat unorthodox, but it can ruin the jump-shooter's effectiveness, especially when he has killed the dribble. Make this approach as close as possible without contact, and harass him as much as possible without fouling him. This same technique can be used to harass a passer who raises the ball above his head to pass after ending a dribble.
5. Fake him, and harass him to get a commitment from him. When he has committed himself on the shot, get a hand in his face, shout at him—disconcert him with voice, hands, and every weapon possible.

Defensing the jump-shooter requires special work and special techniques.

DEFENSIVE CONCEPTS TO STRESS CONTINUOUSLY

In conformity with the previously mentioned basic defensive concepts, the coach should emphasize what might be called the *spice lines* of defense. That something *extra* is always needed to promote defense and a defensive consciousness in every player. Tell the players—*you play defense with your mind, your feet, your body, your hands, your voice, and your entire self*—the whole you.

The mental aspect of defense is very important. The coach should guide the players into mental processes of defensive thinking. Several notable coaches have been excellent examples of coaches that have advocated this process. Each coach will have to find his own method of applying this technique to his players. Research studies have been made comparing the results of improvement made in certain motor skills by mental practice with the actual practice of the skill. Results show that players doing the mental practice of certain motor skills improve almost as much as those actually practicing the skill in certain situations. Certainly this is one phase of the game where the coach can guide mental processes and attitudes to produce a much finer defensive unit.

Some other points of emphasis can be summarized as follows: Switch as little as possible on defense—and then only to give help or assistance to a teammate who is in trouble, or who has made a defensive mistake. A better term to use is *help*, rather than switch. A good slogan for the players to use is, "I'd rather *help* than *switch*."

When playing the man with the ball, the defensive player should say to himself at all times, "He won't go by, he can't get by," and then *never* let him by. A defensive player should *never* let an offensive player with the ball drive the base line. A defensive, fundamental *must* is "seal the baseline." The defensive player should overshift on the man with the ball and force him to the situation desired. The defense should never allow the opponents to have complete freedom on offense. They should, at every opportunity, attempt to dominate, *enslave*, handcuff, and force them into situations where they cannot perform their best.

In making defensive assignments, the coach should match speed against speed, and height against height. The defense should do a lot of sinking, floating, sagging, and two-timing in every situation possible. Attempts should be made to put pressure on the man with the ball, and if he breaks loose, the man in the hole must fill in—the player who lost his opponent must sprint to the inside and pick up on a help situation or the switch.

Every coach will have certain pet ideas he wants his players to believe in. One such pet idea that is fundamentally sound on defense is the concept that nearly all players who are right handed will hurt you the least when forced to go left for a shot, and that left-handed players will hurt you less when forced to go right for a shot. Usually a right-handed player can still hurt you when fading to his right, but will seldom hurt you when forced to fade left, and vice-versa for the left-handed player. Forcing them to move opposite their natural handedness to get off a shot forces an unnatural "cock" of the wrist that must be used in getting off the shot. This type of shot is seldom successful and as a result is not nearly as likely to hurt the defensive team. Thus the basic concept—force the offensive player to go opposite his natural handedness at all times.

DEFENSIVE MISTAKES TO AVOID

Some defensive mistakes are of such magnitude and in such serious violation of fundamental defensive concepts that special emphasis should be given to them and players should constantly be reminded that these errors are to be avoided. Some of them are:

1. Keeping the hands in a high position out on the floor—so high as to take the heel of the back foot off the floor.
2. Taking the original stance against the man with the ball with the feet parallel, or in a square stance, or what is sometimes called a wrestler's stance. The only exceptions to this are when the offensive player has ended his dribble, or is taking the ball up to jump-shoot—then the player may move in *close* with a *wide square stance* to harass the ball handler.
3. Stabbing downward at the ball with the hands, especially where the weight of the body is thrown forward, and where the sole of the back foot comes off the floor. This results in the center of gravity of the body being thrown outside its base causing a lack of stability, and an inability to react properly to a penetrating drive.
4. Leaving the feet or jumping off the floor to knock the ball down on an attempted shot by an opponent. Such an effort seldom accomplishes its purpose, and leaves the player in a defensive position that can be costly. The player can accomplish more with less commitment by keeping proper defensive position and balance.
5. Standing erect, or upright without being in the defensive stance. Such a position simply means the player is not alert, or ready to make the defensive play. He is "out of it."
6. Resting, or loafing on defense. Remember that it requires constant hustle, work, talk, and communication to be a good defensive team.

Constant re-evaluation of methods and techniques by the coach can bring about a determined and effective defensive team.

DRILLS USED TO TEACH INDIVIDUAL DEFENSIVE CONCEPTS

There are countless drills that can be used to teach the individual basic defensive concepts. A few of those that are considered good, and that have proven successful will be diagrammed and explained in the following pages. Each coach may select those that he finds best suited to his particular system and that are adaptable to his "thing."

DIAGRAM 1-2—Drill 1. The formation shown in this diagram can be used to work several drills to teach the mechanics and footwork of the *stance,* the *retreat step,* the *drop step,* and the defensive glide used in defensive play. The leader gets out in front of the players lined up in the formation shown. The leader could be the coach, an assistant coach, or a squad leader. The players face the leader, and take the defensive stance as if guarding the leader with a ball. The stance should be checked to see that the players are in the *boxer's stance,* one foot in front of the other, comfortably spread, with weight evenly distributed over both feet. Hands should be up, arms bent, and about shoulder level. In the first drill, the leader will call the direction of the shift by calling forward, right, left, back, etc., or he may point in the direction of the desired shift, and the players shift in the direction indicated. The leader should start out by doing the drill 3 minutes a day, then increase the time as the season goes along until the players are conditioned to do the drill to a time limit desired by the coach, such as 8 to 12 minutes per day. While doing the drill the coach should check the stance, the footwork, the glide, and the various defensive position techniques.

DIAGRAM 1-2

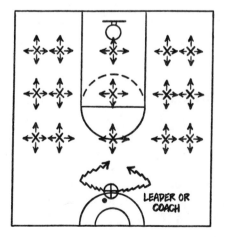

Drill 2—Using the same formation as shown in Diagram 1-2, the leader takes a ball with each player taking a stance as if guarding the leader. It should be announced beforehand whether the leader is right or left handed, and the direction he is to be forced in on his drive. The players take a stance accordingly. If the leader fakes only, the players *retreat step*, and immediately reverse the retreat step into an *attack*. If the leader drives to the side of the open stance, the players *retreat step* and glide with him to counter the move. If the leader drives opposite the direction of the forward foot, the players *retreat step*, then *drop step*, and go into the defensive glide to counter his move. This drill gives the coaches an opportunity to review, and check the mechanics of the footwork of the players to make certain that they make the first moves properly. This drill should be worked in with Drill 1 in timing the work done on this technique each day.

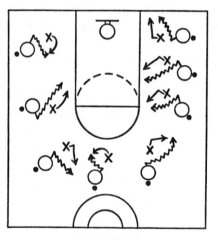

DIAGRAM 1-3

DIAGRAM 1-3—This diagram shows Drill 3. The players pair up and scatter about the floor. One ball is allotted to each pair, and one player takes the ball on the offensive, and the other takes the defensive attack playing one on one against each other. The offensive player tries to dribble around the defensive player, who attacks, or approaches in defensive stance close enough to reach out and touch the man with the ball. The defensive man is to prevent the offensive player with the ball from driving around him. The player with the ball will fake, step back, rocker step, jab, and drive to get the defensive player to commit himself so that he can drive past him or around him. They take turns on offense and defense. The coaches check constantly to perfect the defensive moves—checking the stance, the retreat step, the attack, the drop step, and the glide. If the defensive player makes his first and second moves properly, the offensive player will have a hard time driving around him. The defensive player should practice the overshift principle and experiment with forcing the offensive player in the direction he wants to make him go.

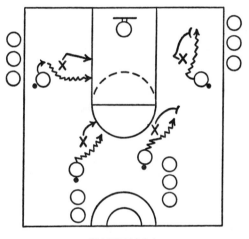

DIAGRAM 1-4

DIAGRAM 1-4—Drill 4. The players position themselves on the floor as shown in the diagram. This is called "one-on-one" from the guard and forward spots. The forward takes the ball in what is called the forward operational area (all players work this spot as well as the guard spot) with his back to the defensive player. The defensive player reaches out and flicks the offensive player across the hips, and that is the signal to start. The offensive player turns, faces his opponent and goes into his individual maneuvers to elude the defensive player. This same drill is worked from the guard operational areas, except that the ball handler does not turn his back to the defensive player. The players rotate spots, and go from offense to defense in each position on the floor. The action is rotated from spot to spot while all the players observe the action with the coach constantly checking the maneuvers. Various games can be used and scores can be kept in a one-on-one contest to motivate the players and to add zip and life to the drill. The "Defensive Drill Man-of-the-Week" could be selected from contests or records kept from the drill, and some reward or honor given each week. To play defense, it is necessary to be able to stop the man with the ball.

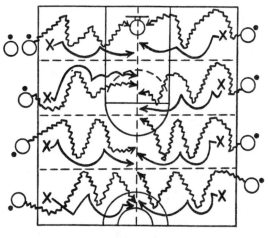

DIAGRAM 1-5

DIAGRAM 1-5—Drill 5. In this diagram, the court is divided into imaginary lines as shown by the dotted lines. In reality this could be termed a two-fold drill—one to work on the dribble, and the other to work on maintaining defensive position on the dribbler. The player with the ball works on the dribble, and dribbles halfway across the court working on the cross-over, change of direction, change of pace, faking, and protecting the dribble in an effort to beat the defensive player. The defensive player just works on maintaining position on the dribbler. He should not slap at the ball with the hands, but should keep one hand down to protect on the cross-over, the other hand up, with the stance open to the side of the dribble, thereby maintaining good defensive position. The players should work first at half speed, and then later at full speed. When the imaginary middle line of the court is reached, the players should change from offense to defense and work back to the side line on the same drill. This drill is called the "Defense and Dribbler Drill."

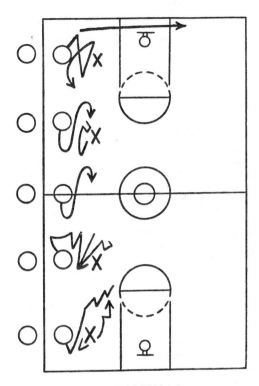

DIAGRAM 1-6

DIAGRAM 1-6—Drill 6. This is another defensive footwork drill. A stop-watch should be used. The players should work for 10 seconds at a slow, warm-up speed. This should be followed with 20 seconds at half speed, then followed with 30 seconds at full speed. The tempo should be changed by the coach's whistle. "0" is the offensive player. "X" is the defensive player. The drill can be executed from the sideline to the middle of the court as shown in the diagram, or it could be worked with fewer players, working from the end line to the mid-court line. The defensive player hooks his thumbs inside his belt, and guards the offensive player without using his hands and arms, learning to stay with 0 using footwork only. 0, the offensive player, makes all the possible maneuvers he can to elude the defensive player by stopping, starting, changing directions, etc., without the ball. The players should take turns on defense and offense. After running the drill with thumbs tucked inside the belt, the drill should be repeated allowing the defense to use the hands and arms along with the feet. The drill may be run with or without the ball. The purpose: Learn to play defense with the feet and the mind.

Other suggestions for drills that will help improve the individual defensive techniques are:

1. Work one against one for the full length of the court.
2. Work two against two from the guard and forward operational areas. Check the defensive work carefully on this drill, and while doing this the coach can teach the individual offensive maneuvers from these spots, which become a part of the regular offense.
3. Work two against two from the guard operational areas. Check the defense constantly, and while doing this build the offense maneuvers from these spots, which become a part of the regular offense.
4. Work three against three from the two guard spots and from one forward operational area. Check the defense constantly while teaching the offensive maneuvers that will be a part of the regular offense from these three operational areas. Be sure to teach how to counter every offensive maneuver that may be encountered.
5. Later, add the fourth and fifth players, incorporating the complete offense and defense in teaching and checking both. While teaching defense, also build the offense.
6. To acquaint the players with pressure situations, run many drills with two against two and three against three, the full court, constantly checking both the defense and the offense. Build on pressure and attack.

Some special drills for teaching the defensive player how to defense the man without the ball need to be incorporated into the coaching, teaching, and work program. The following diagrams give some well-proven possibilities.

DIAGRAM 1-7—In this drill, 01 with the ball passes in to 02 who is defensed or guarded by X2. 02 maneuvers to beat X2. X2 plays his defense in an aggressive manner and makes 02 work hard to get the ball. X2 should play with his inside foot forward, and almost on the line

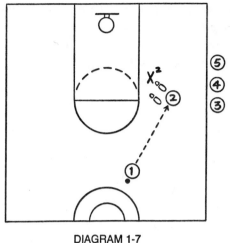

DIAGRAM 1-7

from the ball to his opponent as shown in the diagram. 02 maneuvers to get the ball, and when he does get the ball he maneuvers to beat X2. If 02 gets in trouble or kills the dribble, he may pass back to 01 and start the drill over again. The defensive work of X2 should be constantly checked. In taking the stance or foot position shown, should 02 reverse the back side or baseline side of X2, X2 must turn to the inside, pivoting on the back and outside foot, face the ball, and play to break up the move in this way. Next on offense will be 03. 02 will be the next defensive player. In this drill, the defensive player is drilled on guarding the player with and without the ball.

DIAGRAM 1-8—This is a special drill to teach the defensive player to guard the man without the ball and to learn how to prevent his opponent from receiving the ball. A coach, manager, or another player has the ball as shown in the diagram. 02 on the opposite side of the court maneuvers and breaks toward the ball to get open for a pass. X2 must take a stance that will enable him to see the ball and his opponent 02. He must not let 02 execute a reverse against him, or break into the vital scoring area where he will be able to receive the ball. He can play 02 loosely until 02 approaches the areas where he could receive the ball. X2 should play at the side and in front of 02, if necessary, to prevent him from receiving the ball. At times X2 should face the ball, and screen 02 out of the play in order to keep him from moving to receive a pass. If 02 succeeds in receiving the ball in this area, then X2 defenses him in the best way he can. 02 may pass back to the coach or the outlet man, if he is countered. The players should rotate on offense and defense so that every player has an equal opportunity to participate in the drill.

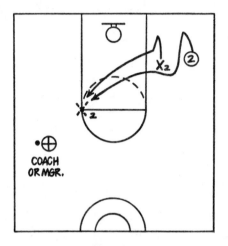

DIAGRAM 1-8

DIAGRAM 1-9—In this drill, two offensive lines are set up as shown in the diagram. The one line headed by 04 is out of bounds on the side of the court. 01 has the ball. X1 is guarding him. 01 passes the ball out of bounds to 04. X1 is expected to react accordingly as 01 passes off. 01 and 04 now maneuver and execute a two-man out-of-bounds play. 01 maneuvers to get open for a pass. X1 plays to prevent him from getting open. X2 is now guarding 04 who has the ball. 04 passes inbounds to 01 at the spots shown in the diagram and then drives for a return pass. As soon as 04 passes inbounds to 01, X2 who is guarding 04 without the ball, must loosen up accordingly, and play to prevent him from receiving a return pass from 01. Later in this drill, the other guard, forward, and center could be included in the drill. The out-of-bounds plays can be developed from the sideline and the appropriate defensive counters could be taught at the same time.

DIAGRAM 1-10—In this drill the offensive players move the ball around from player to player. The defensive players work on properly defensing

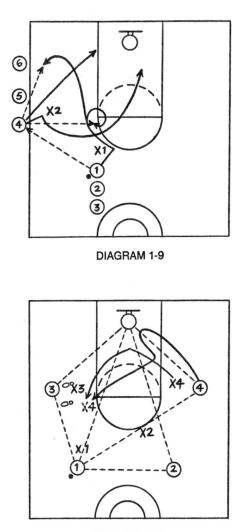

DIAGRAM 1-9

DIAGRAM 1-10

the man with the ball (X1); on defensing properly to make the man on the ball side of the floor work hard to get the ball (X3) (note foot position of X3 shown); and on defensing the weak side player, and not letting him break toward the ball ahead of the defensive man to receive the ball in the scoring area (X4). Note the dotted lines giving the two imaginary lines that the defensive players must be aware of and play to at all times—the line from the opponent to the ball, and the line from the opponent to the basket. When the opponent does not have the ball, the defensive player must make adjustments between these two lines based on the speed of the opponent, distance from the ball, position of the ball, his own speed, speed of opponent's passing and the defensive application being made at the time.

DIAGRAM 1-11

DIAGRAM 1-11—This drill is used to teach X5 to prevent a pass being made to 05 in the close scoring area. Players 01, 02, 03, and 04 pass the ball around rapidly in an effort to get the ball inside to 05. 05 works and maneuvers to get open, but is defensed by X5 who checks, fronts, and sides 05. X5 makes every effort to stay between 05 and the ball and to prevent him from receiving a pass inside the vital scoring area.

THE NUMBERED DEFENSIVE SYSTEM

The basic defensive concepts presented in this chapter will be given different applications in later chapters in this book. These different applications will be in the form of a numbered defensive system. The concepts presented here are necessary for superb defensive play and the numbered defenses will be based on, and in conformity with, these concepts.

The ten basic numbered defenses will be number 10, 20, 30, 40, 11,

12, 13, 31, 31Z and 41. In addition to these basic numbered defenses, optional defenses numbered 10T, 14, 15, 42, 43, and 44 will be presented. These optional defenses may be substituted for any of the basic ten, or added to them as the coach and team may find practical and necessary.

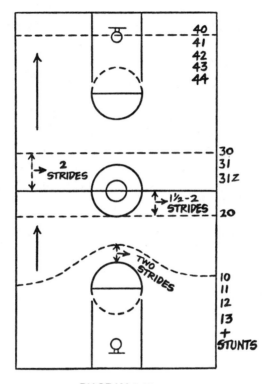

DIAGRAM 1-12

DIAGRAM 1-12—This diagram gives the complete court defensive areas showing the positions on the court where the attack points of the defenses begin, and where they are applied. This simplifies the system and helps the player to realize that he is merely applying the basic defensive concepts at different attack points on the court. Possessing this knowledge and understanding this defensive system make it simple and easy to change the defenses constantly and thus present the offense with a different set of circumstances each time they advance down the floor in the offensive attack. The 10, 11, 12, 13, and other defenses numbered less than 20 begin their attack about two strides in front of the top of the free throw circle, or just back of the now so-called fore-court and mid-court division area. The number 20 defense attack point is about 1½ to 2 strides back of the court division line. Any 30 numbered defense begins the attack just beyond the division line —usually two to three strides over, so as to be a fully effective half-court defense. Any 40 numbered defense is a full-court press and the attack point is shown by the dotted line on the court diagram.

Only the players can have possession of the ball. Only the ball can go through the basket and count for points. Only the player can put it through the basket in order for it to count points on the scoreboard. The focal point of the applications of the basic defensive concepts in this chapter and in all the defensive maneuvers shown and described in this book will be upon the player with the ball. This is where the defensive concentration should be. This is the focal point with any and all defensive play. Stop the player with the ball and the defensive battle is won. It takes the player with the ball to score points—it can't be done any other way. Stop him, and the scoring stops. Defense concentrated in this manner means successful defensive play that leads to basketball victories.

SECTION ONE

The Great Man-to-Man Defenses

2

THE NUMBER 10 DEFENSE:
The Basic Defense

The number 10 defense is the basic defense to be used and is a normal defense within the scoring zone of the opponents. It is the first defense that should be taught and used. (As such it could be referred to as the basic defense.) In this defense the players drop back into the opponent's scoring area as soon as possession of the ball is lost and pick up their assigned men as they come into the scoring area. To establish some basic fundamental principles for the defense, the court is divided into three areas or zones. These areas or zones are referred to as areas A, B, and C as shown in Diagram 2-1.

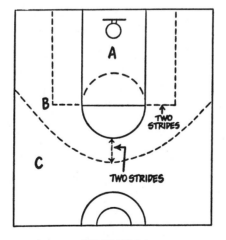

DIAGRAM 2-1

DIAGRAM 2-1—When using the number 10 defense, the defensive end of the court is divided into areas A, B, and C as shown in the diagram. Area A encompasses the vital scoring area and it is often referred to as the pivot-past player operational area. It is identified as the court area from the free throw lane to the base line and extends outward on each side of the free throw lane about two full strides from the free throw line extended. Area A is to be played as a *zone* area. The objective of the defense is never to allow a ball to be passed to an offensive opponent while he is in this area, or at least to knock down 70% of all passes into the area. Play in the area must be rugged and tough. The defense must play in front of and between the opponent and the ball in this area. The defensive player must never, at any time, nor in any situation, allow the opponent to break into this area ahead of him toward the ball. He should always be in front of him toward the ball, and play the ball just as in a *zone* defense. If a high or a floater type of pass is attempted over the defensive player's head, he should be coached to go for the ball in just the same manner as an outfielder goes after a fly ball—as soon as the ball leaves the passer's finger tips, go for it, regardless of everything else. The defensive player guarding the pivot player, or any player in this area should always remember that the weak side floater or sagging defensive players will be there to help him.

Area B begins about two full strides in front of the free throw circle, and encompasses the area outside of area A toward the basket that could be regarded as a normal shooting or scoring range. At times it could begin slightly farther out than this, and at other times, the defense could be moved in to make tighter contact than this distance. Normally, though, the distance will be from about 23 to 26 feet from the basket. It will depend upon the scoring range of the opponents. In area B, the defense plays the point of the ball (the man with the ball) tight and aggressively. The defense should float and sag off from the weak side using a strong zone principle. In guarding at the point of the ball the player should be close enough to lean forward and touch the opponent. He would have to be this close to have him really covered.

Area C is the area of the court out beyond the normal shooting or scoring zone. It is the area of the court beyond the accurate shooting range of the offensive players—usually beyond 23 to 26 feet from the basket. With some players it could be less distance, and with some it could be more. The only thing the defensive player needs to do when in a 10 defense to guard a player in area C is to stay on a line between him and the basket. He should never move out and pressure him unless the player hits from this area and proves to be a dangerous scoring threat. If this is the case, play him tight when he has the ball.

In the number 10 defense there are three basic problems that the defense must be prepared to stop.

1. The first problem is to cover the pivot player or players in area A. The defense must knock down or intercept 70% or more of all passes coming into this area before they can be considered to be doing a decent job.
2. The number two problem is to cover the man at the point of the ball in area B.
3. The number three problem is to cover the drive of the wing player, or the cut of the weak side player moving in toward the ball.

There are four spot situations that the defensive players should be able to take care of in an efficient manner. They are:

1. The cross and roll by the guards. There are very few defensive players who can properly defense this maneuver when it is executed properly. To be able to do so is a step toward better defense.
2. The split the post situation.
3. The pass and go either inside or outside for a screen situation.
4. The sucker play, or the simple pass, and cut.

These are four offensive spot situations for which the defensive players must be well drilled and prepared to stop.

In the number 10 defense the weak side defensive players drop off on a strong sag or float and, by using the overshift with the correct stance, force the offensive players to the middle with their drive, especially the wing players. In forcing them to the middle, the defensive player *must* be ready to go with the opponent into the middle where he will have plenty of help. The defensive player should always cut off the *outside drive*, and be ready to move with the offensive player to the middle. While he is in the middle *gang him*—let him have nothing. A rule or principle of this defense is, "Cut off the outside drive and seal the base-line cut." Then let no one except the Almighty High have anything down the middle. This rule or principle of forcing everything toward the middle to take advantage of the ganging defense is called "The Number 10 Principle." This principle will be referred to in the discussion of other defenses in later chapters. It can be used as a variation to the other defenses where the basic forcing principles require that the offensive players be forced to the outside. By applying the 10 principle to other defenses, another variable can be added to all the defenses.

Concerning the baseline drive—it is an absolute must that no opponent be allowed to drive the baseline. It must be sealed off completely. This is in conformity with the overshift principle of forcing the opponent to the middle where help can be secured. If the opponent is able to get around the defensive player along the baseline, he is in a position where the defensive player can secure no help. The offensive player can now exploit one of three very good options in this situation. They are:

1. He can drive all the way, and come in from behind the basket for a good scoring opportunity.
2. If a teammate leaves his opponent in area A to help his defensive teammate who allowed the opponent to drive the baseline, the offensive player will dump a bounce pass to a teammate right in front of the basket for a fine scoring opportunity.
3. If the offensive player is allowed to drive the baseline, he can drive to a point midway along the baseline, stop, and execute a jump-shot for an easy two points the way players shoot today.

No player should ever allow the opponent to drive past him along the baseline.

DIAGRAM 2-2—The basic idea of the weak side float or sag is shown in this diagram. 02 has the ball. X2 guards him tight at the point of the ball. X4 plays 04 in such a manner as to make him work to get the ball. Defensive players X1 and X3 sag into the middle. They play almost a zone principle, but must drop straight back on an imaginary line from their opponent to the basket. They will then make adjustments considering an imaginary line from the ball to their opponent, and make an adjustment between these two lines so that they always keep their man and the ball in view. X1 must learn how far he can float or move away from his opponent. He must make sure he can quickly advance to the attack position on 01, should 02 pass him the ball. X5 plays in front of 05 and between him and the ball, since 05 is in area A. Should a floater

DIAGRAM 2-2

pass be attempted over X5's head, X3 is responsible for the area behind him and he must give help from the weak side. X3's float is con-
siderable, and again is determined by his speed, his opponent's speed,
and how fast the opponents move the ball. He must be sure he knows
where his man is (03 in this case) and where the ball is. He is responsible for the dotted area behind him, should a teammate lose his man,
and should he break open into this area. He must always make sure
that 03 never breaks into area A ahead of him toward the ball—always
being ready to front him, and step in front of him to block him out. The
front line on the number 10 defense must not be parallel at any time, as
shown by the positions of X2 and X1 in the diagram.

DIAGRAM 2-3—This diagram shows how X5 should play if 05 breaks
high to meet a pass in the outer half of the free throw circle. X5 in this
case will front and side him. X3 is responsible for high passes over 05's
head, should 02 float a pass into this area to beat X5 in his effort to cut
off passes to 05.

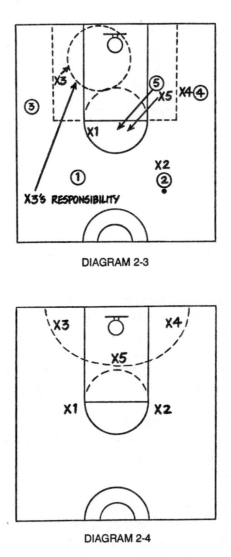

DIAGRAM 2-3

DIAGRAM 2-4

DIAGRAM 2-4—When the offense puts up a shot, the defensive players form a cup as shown in this diagram. They should not allow themselves to be forced underneath the basket. If forced too far underneath, their rebounding efforts will be ineffective. Two players then go after the ball wherever it comes off the board on the rebound, while the other three move into the lanes to set up the fast break pattern.

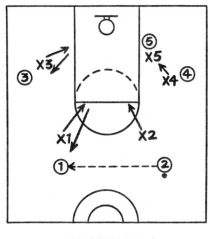

DIAGRAM 2-5

DIAGRAM 2-5—X1 must learn how far to sag off so that he can cover 01 if the pass is made to him as shown in the diagram. X2 drops off into the hole as shown, when 02 passes the ball to 01 or when he passes off. X2 should not turn his back, but should drop straight back in order to keep both the man and the ball in view. X3 and X4 will also vary their positions as movement of the ball is made. When the ball moves from 02 to 01, X3 will tighten his position on 03 and make him work to get the ball. Now X4 can slide off 04 and will be responsible for the deep areas behind 05, should he advance to meet the ball.

DIAGRAM 2-6—If the offense decides to put up a shot to give 05 the inside rebound position because of the way X5 plays in front of him, then X3 should move in quickly from the weak side to block 05 off the boards. X5 should cross over to the opposite side to cover the rebound area on the side vacated by X3. X4 will block out and cover to the right side, and as a result, the rebound areas will have the usual coverage.

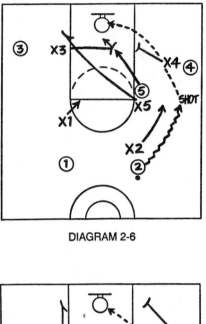

DIAGRAM 2-6

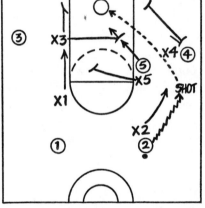

DIAGRAM 2-7

DIAGRAM 2-7—Another way in which the situation described in Diagram 2-6 could be covered is shown in this diagram. As 02 starts his dribble to the right to put up the shot to give 05 the inside position on the rebound, X1 moves deeper toward the basket. As the shot is put up by 02, X1 covers the rebound position on the left side while X3 crosses over to block out 05. X5 then takes the position in front of the basket on the rebound cup. X4 blocks out as usual.

DIAGRAM 2-8—When the guard 02 passes and cuts for an outside screen as shown in this diagram, X4 steps back and calls for a *slide through*. X2 will slide through as shown if 02 is a poor shooter and has not demonstrated that he can shoot effectively from a position in front of 04. X2 will slide between X4 and 04 picking up 02 as he comes around 04. X2 and X4 should talk constantly while this move is being executed so as to be sure they have the calls correct. The chief responsibility for the talking is placed upon X4.

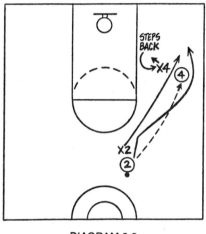

DIAGRAM 2-8

DIAGRAM 2-9—If 02 is a good shot from the side, or if the play is executed at a point and place from where 02 might stop and receive the ball from 04 as he cuts outside and thus be in an effective scoring range, then X2 must fight over the top and play 02 tight as shown in this diagram. X4 should drop off just a little. If 02 should reverse his direction and rub X2 off on 04, then X4 should step up quickly to help and take 02, with X2 rolling quickly to get position on 04. It takes constant alertness, helping, and shifting to prevent rub-off screens in these situations. Lots of talking and helping each other will get the job done.

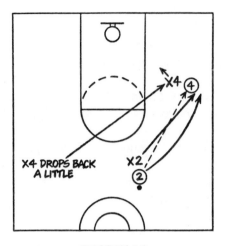

DIAGRAM 2-9

DIAGRAM 2-10—On the guard cross play outside the circle X2 should slide through the screen as X1 drops back as shown in this diagram. X2 will slide between X1 and 01. Constant talk between X1 and X2 will keep it true. X1 may need to drop back just a little to let X2 through. If 02 is an effective shooter from this area, X2 will fight over the top and stick tight to 02, rather than slide through. In fighting through in this situation when he goes over the top, X2 should fight to take the pass or to tie up the ball.

DIAGRAM 2-10

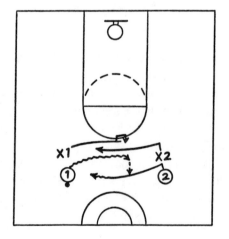

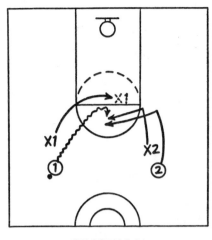

DIAGRAM 2-11

DIAGRAM 2-11—If the guard cross occurs inside the circle as shown in this diagram, and close enough to the basket so that 01 and 02 are in dangerous scoring territory, X2 must fight his way *over the top* and in the path as shown here. If 02 reverses him or picks X2 off, X1 must help by taking 02, and X2 must quickly roll into position to guard 01. Again this calls for a hard-fighting, fast-talking, and a constant-hustling situation.

DIAGRAM 2-12—In playing 05, the pivot man, as shown in this diagram, X5 should front him, and play him loosely, and about one to one-half step from him if possible. The defense must keep successful passes from being made into area A, where 05 is playing. If the ball is thrown over the head of X5 then he should play it as an outfielder plays a fly ball. He must go for the ball. Then X3 and X4, the floaters and saggers, should help out on the overhead pass—they too go for the ball and check 05 out so that he cannot get to the ball. With the weak side floaters coming in to help on this situation, the defense should have no trouble fronting players such as 05 in area A.

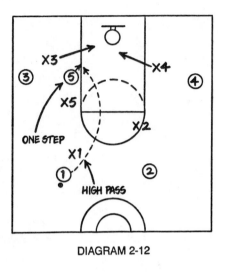

DIAGRAM 2-12

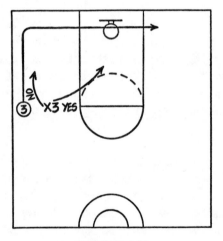

DIAGRAM 2-13

DIAGRAM 2-13—If the player in the position of 03, as shown in this diagram, should reverse X3 or get a start on him to the baseline, or to his rear, then X3 should turn as indicated to head 03 off and prevent passes from being made to him. If he turns to his right as indicated on the *no* arrow, he automatically loses one step on 03 and is immediately behind him. In addition, he has turned his back to the ball, and has lost vision on the passer and the ball. He should turn to the inside as indicated by the arrow marked *yes*. This way he is open to watch the ball, the passer, and to cut corners on 03's drive. This will put him in a position to front the opponent, and check block him on other moves he might make to receive the ball in area A.

DIAGRAM 2-14

DIAGRAM 2-14—In the number 10 defense, the principle of the over-shift is based upon the idea that weak side floaters and saggers will help jam the middle, and that all offensive drives are to be forced to the middle to secure this help. Forcing to the middle is referred to as *"The Number 10 Principle."* The defense should never allow a player to drive down the outside and along the baseline as X3 has done in the diagram. The defensive player should overshift and drive him to the middle as X4 has done on the right side. When he moves to the middle, then the defensive player should go with him tough, and be prepared to get a declaration from him when help is secured.

DIAGRAM 2-15—When the offense executes an inside screen play as shown in this diagram, X1 goes with his opponent 01, the screener, and then loosens up slightly in order to be able to stop the roll-off man. X1 is not the player being screened, and should do most of the talking on the play, calling the move for X3, warning him, etc. X1 should depend on X3 fighting his way over the top or in and around the screen in such a way that he will not be caught or picked. He should go over the top with the dribbler if at all possible, but if this is not possible, he should slide through between X1 and his opponent 01. In either case, he should never be far from 03 and should be able to defense him at all times.

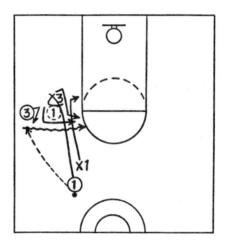

DIAGRAM 2-15

DIAGRAM 2-16—If X3 is consistently being picked or screened out on this inside screen by the offense, then the defensive players X1 and X3, talking constantly, go into a help situation. When X1 follows 01 to the screening situation, he loosens up, and when 03 starts his dribble off the screen, X1 steps out and takes him. As this is being done, X3 steps back and slides into a position that will enable him to move with 01 should he do a roll-off move. There is danger, however, that 03 might reverse back again, but constant talk between the two defensive men should get an early declaration from the dribbler, and they should be able to keep the help situation straightened out. Remember, this help-switch should be made only when X3 is not able to fight his way over the top, or slide through on the screen. The terms "help" and "switch" are a matter of semantics, but "help" seems to convey the idea better.

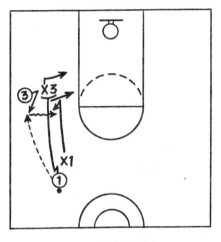

DIAGRAM 2-16

DIAGRAM 2-17—A situation that becomes very difficult for some players to defense is the pick and roll from behind. What makes this difficult to defense is the fact that the pick comes constantly from the rear of the defensive player. When the screen occurs in tight, as shown in this diagram, the defensive man not being screened (in this case X2) calls to his teammate constantly to be alert. X1, in shifting with the dribbler, can watch to the side, and with hands feel to the rear, jitterbugging in and out on him, and then fight through over the top. He may need to make himself thin to go over the top, but he can do it. When he fights through, there is no problem.

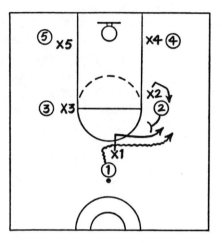

DIAGRAM 2-17

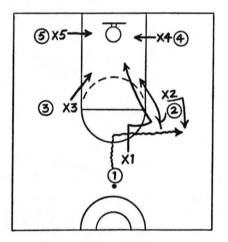

DIAGRAM 2-18

DIAGRAM 2-18—In case X1 should be picked off on the screen by 02, then X2 calls the "help" signal and steps up to take the dribbler. X1 now sprints to the basket to get position on 02, should 02 roll for the basket. The weak side defensive men should also float to help on this roll-off play. In this case X4 and X5 should be looking to help jam the middle on this type of play.

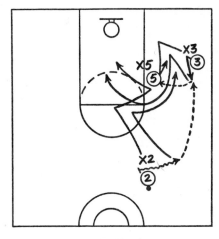

DIAGRAM 2-19

DIAGRAM 2-19—One of the difficult situations to defense is the *split the post* move as shown in this diagram. 02 has passed to 03, and 03 passes into 05 and then 02 and 03 maneuver a "split" move over the top of 05 so as to bump their defensive men into 05 or into each other as 02 and 03 cross close and tight over 05. As usual, X2 and X3 are instructed to fight in close and tight over the top. X5, the man not screened, and the one guarding 05 will call the play and talk constantly. As 02 and 03 cross in front of 05, the greatest danger to X2 and X3 is bumping each other so that they are out of the play, as they fight over the top. What they should do is fight through until they touch each other with outstretched hands, and then they call "help," "I'll take this man," etc. X2 will actually take 03 off the screen, and X3 will take 02. X5 will stay with 05 and be ready to help either of the other players as needed, or to take a free man out of the melee. Constant talking, helping and hustling by all three men should get the defensive job done.

DIAGRAM 2-20—With the pivot post players playing positions as shown here, the defensive players play on the side toward the ball. This is done with the assumption that there will be weak side floaters that can drop in to help in the areas behind the defensive men X5 and X4, in case there are high floater passes made over their heads. If weak side floaters are not in position to give help to the rear, then X5 and X4 should play less to the side, and more to the rear.

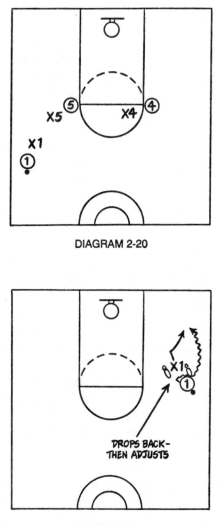

DIAGRAM 2-20

DIAGRAM 2-21

DIAGRAM 2-21—If 01 drives the front foot and leg of X1, and against the side of the open stance, as shown here, X1 does a retreat step and then adjusts with a drop step and goes with him to seal off the base line.

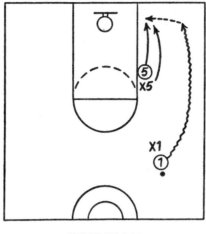

DIAGRAM 2-22

DIAGRAM 2-22—This diagram shows a move that should never happen. The defense must prevent this from happening. As 01 dribbles down in this move, or as the ball is moved in the areas shown, X5 must be on the side toward the ball, making adjustments in his position as the ball moves. This calls for constant adjustment on his part.

DIAGRAM 2-23—In this situation, X1 must never come up behind 01 in area A, or trail him as he comes up in this area toward the ball. X1 should take the path marked *yes*, and be prepared to cut 01 off on his moves toward the ball and be in front of him, as shown in the diagram. If X1 should take the guarding path marked *no*, he will be trailing 01 and come up behind him in a movement toward the ball. He must never allow this to happen.

The Number 10 Defense, while basically a man-to-man defense, nevertheless uses many *zone principles*. It could be considered to be *zonish*, in that it incorporates floating, sagging, sinking, and help tactics that involve zone principles. All emphasis is on the man with the ball. The defensive men guarding an offensive man without the ball must play their man through the ball—in other words, play both the man and the ball. All defensive players must be instilled with the basic

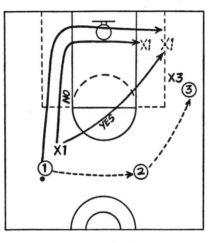

DIAGRAM 2-23

philosophy that everybody helps the defensive teammate guarding the *man with the ball*. To this extent, the defense becomes very *zonish*.

It is also basic in the defensive systems explained in these pages that any zone defense that is used will be very *mannish*. The man with the ball is the threat. He must be stopped. Players who are in scoring areas where they can receive the ball and as a result become a threat must be guarded closely. This explains what is meant by the mannish feature of the zone defenses. The combined principles of both the zone and the man-to-man defenses is what makes a defense tough. The man-to-man defenses will need to be *zonish* and the zone defenses will need to be *mannish*. This really implies that the defenses are never a pure zone or a pure man-to-man defense—that in order for the man-to-man defense to be effective it must be *zonish*, and in order for any zone defense to be effective, it must be *mannish*. This is to say that the man-to-man defenses will use zone principles, and the zone defenses will use man-to-man principles. In fact, if when the team is playing a man-to-man defense they can play zone principles to such an extent that the opponents think they are playing against a zone, and play it as such, this is a mark of success in defensive play.

THE NUMBER 20 DEFENSE:
Pressure to the Outside

The number 20 defense is the first pressing defense to be used and is the beginning of the pressing defensive series. It is basically a man-to-man defense, but uses many zone principles. In the 20 defense, the areas or points where the opponents are picked up are indicated in Diagram 3-1.

DIAGRAM 3-1—The real contact is about two strides back of the center court division line. Actually the defensive players in some instances would wait at the court division line for the advance of the offensive players with the ball, and then retreat from one to one-half steps in making the pressure contact on the offense.

The number 20 defense should be used when playing against a team using a patterned offense, or when the pivot-post player causes more than the usual trouble in the number 10 defensive situation. By applying the pressure just back of the court division line, the offensive team will be forced to abandon their usual patterns, and bring the pivot-post player and the forwards to higher positions where all will be less effective. It will also bring about a change in the offensive tempo —which is just what is needed at times to spoil the timing of the offensive team play. This maneuver may be just enough to render them less effective and will work to the advantage of the defensive team.

As soon as the pressure defenses are begun, the overshift is played differently. The weak side defensive players will no longer float or sag to the extent that they can help jam the middle. In the 20 defense, the

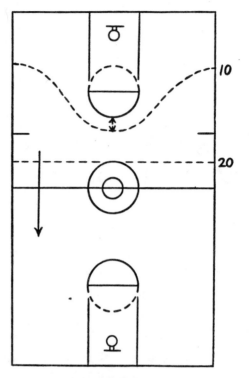

DIAGRAM 3-1

overshift is played so as to force the offensive players to the outside. With the defense applied farther from the basket, it will be advantageous to force the offensive moves to the outside to take the longer distances toward the basket, in most situations. The defense will have more time to recover when the longer route to the outside is taken. The advantages derived from the help that comes from "ganging" to the inside is not available in the 20 defense to the extent that it is in the 10 defense. Forcing the defense to the *outside* in this situation is called *"The 20 Principle."* The "10 principle" and the "20 principle" can be applied in any of the defenses in order to give variety and an added variable. Basically, however, the 20 defense forces the offense to the outside, although the 10 principle can also be applied to the 20 defense. This can be used in situations where the guards cross, and ganging and two-timing tactics can be applied on the dribbler. It can also be used in situations where scouting reports reveal that an opponent may be weaker on a drive opposite his natural movement.

The rules of basketball today have favored the 20 defense. Recent rules changes have divided the front court into mid-court and fore-court areas. A team's mid-court is that part of its front court between the division line and a parallel imaginary line 28 feet from the inside edge of the end boundary to the nearer edge of the mid-court area marker. This imaginary line is located by two three-feet lines, two inches wide measured from the inside edge of each side boundary, and drawn at right angles to it. The rules further state that a held ball occurs when a closely guarded player situated in his mid-court area dribbles, or combines dribbling and holding the ball for five seconds. A continuous count of five seconds on a closely guarded player dribbling the ball, holding the ball, or on a player who has combined dribbling and holding the ball in the mid-court area will result in a jump ball. This is an advantage to the defense and especially to the 20 defense since the mid-court area is where this particular defense starts its pressure tactics. This rule should be exploited by the defense since all they have to do to get a jump ball is to closely guard a player with the ball for five seconds. It adds another trap possibility for the defense, and will give the added pressure to the offense of feeling the necessity for moving the ball past the mid-court area into the fore-court area.

DIAGRAM 3-2—This diagram shows the players in the 20 defense. They pick up their opponents just as they cross the court division line and apply pressure in the mid-court area. X1 plays 01 who has the ball, very tight and close. If 01 is dribbling, X1 will try to stop him and attempt to keep him closely guarded. If he is able to stop 01, he has two things going for him—time, and the pressure 01 feels to get rid of the ball before the five-second count brings about a held ball. X1 will try to permit only a lob pass or a bounce pass by 01. This results in easier interceptions. Pressure by X1 on 01 can cause 01 to pass the ball where it can be picked off by a teammate. While X1 plays 01 tight and aggressive, if 01 should pass the ball behind X1, he must be ready to retreat to areas behind him and help out his teammates. X2 should play 02 tight, and force him outside and away from the ball. X4 should play 04 tight, aggressively, and should play for interceptions. X3 should play 03 tight and aggressive, but must also be responsible for the area behind him. He should be conscious of the responsibility of helping out teammates who may lose their man while moving into this particular area. X5 should front 05 and force him to move in high to receive the ball. When 05 moves in to a high post position, X5 should front him as long as possible, and then drop to the side-front position toward the ball.

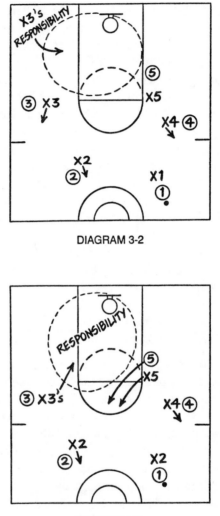

DIAGRAM 3-2

DIAGRAM 3-3

DIAGRAM 3-3—This diagram further illustrates the 20 defense and how X5 would play 05 should he break out to a high post position to receive the ball. One of the purposes of the defense is to get 05 to pull away from area A. However, X5 should still pressure him to the side, front, and toward the ball. The big difference between the 10 defense and the 20 defense is in the play of X3 who is the far weak side defensive player. X3 is responsible for the territory behind him (indicated by dotted circle area). Physically, X3 plays his man tight, but mentally he must always be ready to guard the area behind him. He should be ready to pick up any player who may be lost by his teammate coming into this area near the basket. X1 and X2 should force the play. X4 and X5 should play their men tight and play for interceptions. Such aggressiveness can result in their opponents reversing their direction, cutting behind them and breaking into the area shown in the diagram. X3 must be ready to move both ways, playing interceptions and giving help in the area behind him to prevent the cheap basket. He must be the stopgap in this area. When X1 forces the play, X2 must not let O2 get behind him. In most situations, while using the 20 defense, the defense forces the opponents toward the outside and the sidelines. However, occasionally a 20 defense can be used with a "10 principle" applied. In this situation, the offensive guards would be forced to the middle in order to two-time a dribbler coming off a cross and roll maneuver and because a particular offensive player would be more inept in making this move.

DIAGRAM 3-4—This diagram shows the several trap areas possible by use of the 20 defense. In the areas labeled number 1, the defensive player should, whenever possible, drive or force the dribbler to these areas and force him to stop the dribble here. These are excellent harassing areas and the ball handler can panic, throw a bad pass that can be intercepted, or lose the ball because of a violation of the five-second rule. The areas labeled number 2 are new areas made possible by the new division between mid-court and fore-court. By forcing the dribbler to the outside, the defensive player can trap or get the dribbler to kill his dribble in this area where he is now in a dilemma because of the continuous five-second count. This should be exploited by the 20 defense at every opportunity.

The trap area shown in the diagram and labeled number 3 is an area situated in the mid-court. Traps and two-timing situations can be exploited in this area especially when the guards cross, or when they can be forced into a cross and a hand-off play. When this happens, the two defensive men switch immediately to the player receiving the ball on the hand-off, which has resulted from the cross maneuver. With the umbrella of two defensive men suddenly upon him in this area, the offensive player can, in panic, throw a bad pass that can be intercepted, or he can find himself in a five-second jump-ball situation.

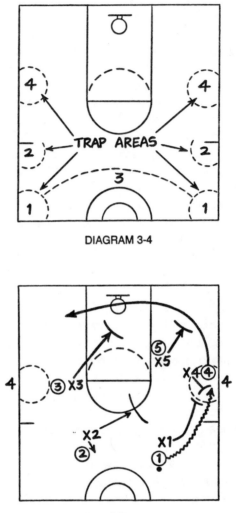

DIAGRAM 3-4

DIAGRAM 3-5

DIAGRAM 3-5—In the trap area labeled number 4, players X1 and X4 team up to two-time the dribbler 01, who has been driven to the outside as shown. If the play is executed on the opposite side of the floor, it would involve X2 and X3. As X1 drives the dribbler 01 toward the sideline into the area labeled number 4, X4 watches his opportunity, fakes a movement to guard 04, and then suddenly jumps out and stops 01 in his dribble as shown in the diagram. X4 and X1 attempt to two-time 01 to force the jump ball or to force him to make a bad pass that can be intercepted. X3 should now be aware of this action, and along with X5 make fake movements to cover their defensive men. Instead they drop into the area behind 05 and 03 to pick up such players as 04 who might have maneuvered themselves free for a pass. At the same time, they, along with X2, should be alert to snag any passes that 01 might throw while in the dilemma of being two-timed.

The number 20 defense is the beginning of the pressure that the defense will exert upon the offense. It will, in many instances, give the defense the clue as to how well the offense will stand up under pressure attack. From these clues the defense will know how to proceed in the next phases of the game.

4

THE NUMBER 30 DEFENSE:
Increase the Pressure

The second pressure defense to be discussed and illustrated is the number 30 defense. This is a tight, aggressive, man-to-man defense. However, it does incorporate zone principles along with some help and switching techniques from all players to the extent that it becomes very *zonish*. It differs from the 20 defense mainly in the point of contact with the offense on the court. The 30 defense meets the offense at a point two to three strides in front of the court division line. The usual procedure is for the front line of the defense to wait at the division line and then, as the ball is brought up the court, the defense advances out in front of the line to initiate the attack. The point of the attack should be two to three full strides in advance of the division line. By beginning the attack at this point, the defense introduces another pressure element to be applied against the offense—that of advancing the ball across the division line within ten seconds. If the offensive team has consumed most or even part of the allotted ten-second time limit before advancing the ball to this area, to be suddenly confronted with defensive pressure and opposition at this point could bring panic. This sudden confrontation could give the defense the tool that it needs to bring about a turnover. The defense should exploit the corner areas next to the division line in every manner possible. Also, by forcing the guards to cross and by using two-timing tactics in the back court, ball turnovers can be forced upon the offense.

Ordinarily the 30 defense operates using the ''20 principle''—that of forcing the offensive player to the outside and toward the sidelines. However, the ''10 principle,'' if applied properly, can force the guards into crossing moves that can result in the kind of back-court situations that are conducive to turnovers. The outside move can be used to force the offensive player into corners at the division line. These corners are referred to as *coffin corners*. These are excellent trap areas that should be exploited at every opportunity.

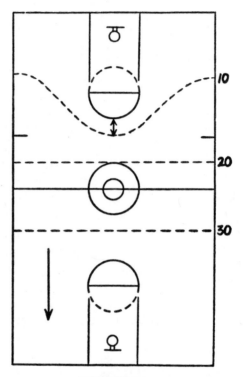

DIAGRAM 4-1

DIAGRAM 4-1—This diagram shows the application point of the 30 defense. The defense pressures the offense as they approach the ten-second court-division line. The coffin corners are to be used to trap the dribbler at every opportunity. The defense should force the ball handler to kill the dribble in the back court if at all possible. When the opponent ends his dribble, the defense should put pressure on him to get rid of the ball quickly. Tie him up if possible. Make him throw the ball somewhere, and permit him to use only the lob or the bounce pass. While the defense is pressuring the ball handler, the defensive teammates should work hard for interceptions.

When a quick two-timing situation is in evidence it should be exploited. This is not to be interpreted to mean that a ball chaser should completely leave his man to go for two-timing situations. The defense should take advantage of opportunities when they are incidental. This means that in carrying out normal defensive duties, if the defensive player finds himself in a close situation where he can pursue a two-timing situation and still have a reasonable chance to recover and guard his opponent, then he should attempt it.

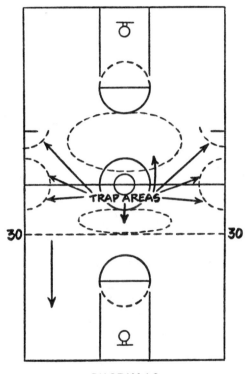

DIAGRAM 4-2

DIAGRAM 4-2—This diagram points out the various trap area possibilities with the application of the 30 defense. If the dribbler can be forced into the corner just prior to crossing the ten-second division line, the pressure will be the greatest while he is in this area. However, he can still find himself in a trap dilemma if he kills his dribble while he is in one of the other indicated areas. He always has the five-second count against him in the mid-court area. The mid-court division line provides another trap area possibility. By applying the "10 principle," trap possibilities are available in the dotted circle areas when the guards handling the ball are forced into a guard cross maneuver. This is one situation in which the two defensive guards can quickly switch to the player receiving the ball while the hand-off from the cross movement is being executed. It involves some risk, but it is usually worth it. In addition, the maneuver is being executed far enough down court so that the defense can usually recover in time to prevent the offense from scoring a cheap basket if the trap does not succeed.

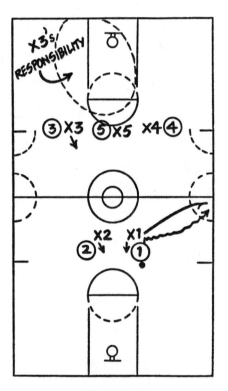

DIAGRAM 4-3

DIAGRAM 4-3—This diagram illustrates where the 30 defense is to make contact with the offense. This should be two to three strides in advance of the ten-second court-division line. Using a "20 principle" X1 forces 01, the dribbler, to the outside and toward the trap areas in the coffin corners. X1's most vigorous effort must be made in this area in order to get 01 to stop the dribble. X1 can accomplish this by getting ahead of him in the direction in which he is dribbling. 01 is now facing the expiration of the ten-second time limit in getting the ball to the front court. If he succeeds in getting across the division line into the next corner and X1 can stop him at this point, he now has a five-second count on him. Actually, in this situation, the sideline and the division line are as effective as teammates in helping X1 trap 01. This dilemma could cause 01 to throw the ball somewhere in desperation or risk a jump ball situation.

X2 should play 02 tight and force him away from the ball. He must, however, be sure 02 does not get behind him. X4, X5, and X3 should also play their men tight and try for interceptions. With the ball in the position shown in the diagram, X3 must play the same as in the 20 defense. He must play physically tight on 03. He must also be responsible for the area to the rear of X5 and X4. He must always be mentally alert to prevent a cheap basket that might come as a result of an offensive player reversing his direction or breaking into this area. X5 should play high and in front of 05. X4 and X3 should always play so as to make 04 and 03 work to get the ball. They should also try for possible interceptions when 01 makes careless passes as he very well may do under pressure.

DIAGRAM 4-4—This diagram illustrates how X1 and X2 work constantly to drive the dribbler, either 01 or 02, to the best possible trap areas. In these areas the defensive players take advantage of the sidelines, the ten-second division, and the mid-court division markers. These advantages are almost as valuable to him in the way of defensive help as is a teammate.

DIAGRAM 4-4

DIAGRAM 4-5

DIAGRAM 4-5—Sometimes a very quick two-timing situation can be worked from this defense in the trap areas as shown in the diagram. In case X1 is not able to establish a position that would force 01 to end his dribble, should 04 linger near the area, then X4 could jump in to stop the dribbler. X4, along with X1, could now throw a two-timing umbrella over him. The five-second count is now in effect, and 01 could be in serious trouble. X5 and X3 should make quick position adjustments to prevent the cheap basket. They should also play for possible pass interceptions.

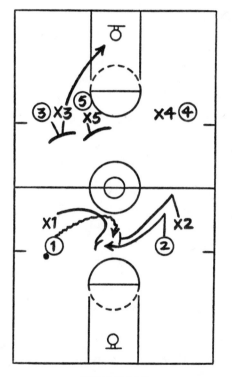

DIAGRAM 4-6

DIAGRAM 4-6—The "10 principle" can be used in the 30 defense, especially on the guards who will do a cross move when forced to the middle. When the dribbler crosses as shown in this diagram, X1 and X2 two-time the guard 02 who receives the ball on the cross from 01. X1 attacks low, and X2 comes in at him high with hands up. The defensive players X3, X4, and X5 play high and work hard for possible pass interceptions. Both X3 and X4 must be held responsible for the area underneath the basket.

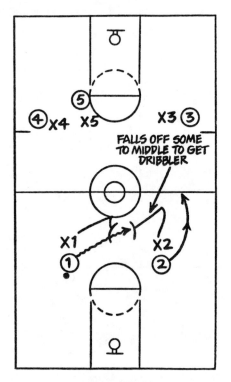

DIAGRAM 4-7

DIAGRAM 4-7—Sometimes in the 30 defense when using the "10 principle" a quick two-timing situation can be exploited when the guards do not cross. As X1 drives the dribbler 01 toward the middle, X2 falls off some and to the inside. Sometimes a quick two-timing situation on the dribbler can be worked, or the dribbler may drive into trouble.

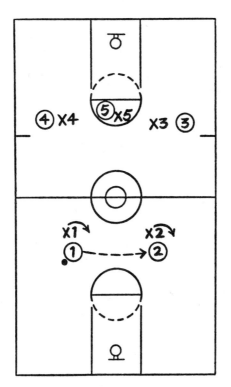

DIAGRAM 4-8

DIAGRAM 4-8—In working the "10 principle" in the 30 defense, the two guards can keep maneuvering and changing their positions in order to drive the ball handler to the inside. For instance, if the ball should be moved from 01 to 02 as shown in the diagram, the defensive players should shift their positions. This move will force the play in the desired direction and to the inside.

DIAGRAM 4-9—The defensive players should never chase the ball to the extent that X2 leaves his man and goes chasing the ball as shown in the diagram. Instead, the defensive players should work to force the dribbler into trap areas to the outside, or into a cross move where quick two-timing situations can be obtained.

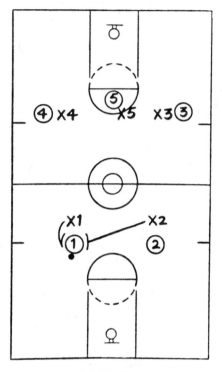

DIAGRAM 4-9

5

THE NUMBER 40 DEFENSE:
Full-court Pressure

The number 40 defense is a full-court pressing defense. While it is basically a man-to-man type of defense, the 40 defense, like the 20 and the 30 defenses, also uses zone principles. This means that there will be many "help" and "switching" situations occurring that will require player cooperation in defensing certain maneuvers. The main objective of the defense is to keep pressure on the player with the ball at all times. This means constant pressure extending over the entire court from end-line to end-line. All defensive players must always be constantly alert to the pressure of their teammate who is guarding the man with the ball. They must be able at any time to assist him, should his pressure tactics bring about a defensive error that would allow the offensive player to get past him or outmaneuver him. As in other pressure defenses, when a quick two-timing situation occurs, it should be taken advantage of immediately. The strong side players should always look for double-teaming possibilities. The weak side players should look for possibilities of pass interceptions.

Some of the basic ideas of the pressure defenses will be further discussed in this chapter since the 40 defense is in reality a full-court pressure defense, and as such, it should make complete use of, and initiate all the pressure principles of this type of defense. The players should be thoroughly grounded in and taught all the fundamentals used in executing the full-court man-to-man pressing defense. This should be done before they are taught to use the zone pressing defenses that will be explained in detail in later chapters of this book.

In using all of the pressing defenses, the defense should not press to the extent that they will commit a foul, or let the opponent get past them or outmaneuver them. The defense should harass and apply as much pressure as possible without making a mistake. For them to commit a foul or let an opponent get past them is a mistake that must be avoided at all costs.

In order to use this type of defense, the players must be alert and ready to react instantly in all situations. They must learn to develop the ability to anticipate what the ball handler is going to do next. If the defensive team is blessed with player talent that is also sparked by aggressiveness, initiative, pride, poise, and patience it will greatly add to the effectiveness of the defense.

The first duty of the defense is to stop the dribbler and force him to make a bad pass which in turn will result in an interception. It should be remembered that in basketball there are *throwers* and there are *passers*. This is the type of situation where the defense wants to force all the opponents to be *throwers*. If the offense makes a mistake, the defense should capitalize upon it whenever possible. The entire idea of the pressure defenses, and especially the 40 defense, is not necessarily to take the ball away from the opponent, but rather to pressure them to such an extent as to cause them to lose possession of the ball. The purpose of the press is to upset the usual pattern of play and force the offense into situations with which they are not familiar.

The 40 defense will pick up the opponents no later than the back court (offensive) free throw line extended. At times the defense should attempt to intercept the first pass, and in doing so should place great pressure on the player who is taking the ball out of bounds. When this is done, the defensive players should spread their hands and arms wide and try to force the player making the throw-in to make a high pass and possibly a long one. The defense should encourage the high, long pass or the bounce pass. The defense should encourage passes to certain areas by baiting the offense with what appears to be an obvious pass opening.

There are times when the players using the 40 defense will not bother to guard the player taking the ball out of bounds. When this is done, one defensive player should be dropped into the middle of the court near the front-court (offensive back-court) free throw line for the purpose of zoning and also to help two-time an opponent for a brief period of time. He should maintain this position until the ball has been thrown inbounds, and the player making the throw-in has moved onto the court. Instead of harassing the thrower-in, this player, by dropping off into the previously described position, will expect to gain more by playing for pass interceptions as well as helping to create two-timing situations that will result in ball possession for his team. In playing this situation, he must never allow himself to be maneuvered or drawn so far from the action that he will not be in a position to guard the thrower-in when he moves onto the court after he makes the pass inbounds.

When an all-court press such as the 40 defense is used, the defense is as effective as the weakest player. If one player does not press, or for any reason is not in a position to apply the necessary pressure, then he nullifies the efforts of the entire team. As a result, the four other players' efforts are minimized, because for the 40 defense to be successful all five players must work together as a complete unit.

There are two ways to use the 40 defense, and the material available will be the determining factor as to which one will be used. The first way is to have all the players assigned to guard specific opponents. They pick up their assigned man as early as possible, using in the meantime as many help situations and switching combinations as can be used to apply as much pressure on the player in possession of the ball as possible. In the other method, no defensive assignments should be made. Two players should be assigned to cover the back court area as soon as the opponents gain possession of the ball. They sprint back to pick up the first offensive players breaking down the court. If there are no offensive men breaking down the court, then these two defensive players go no further down floor than the court division line. From this position they can move back on defense and help their teammates apply pressure on the offense as needed. No defensive assignments should be made in this situation. The defensive players pick up the nearest opponent as soon as possession of the ball is lost, except for the two players who are held responsible for the back court area as described previously. This maneuver will require a great amount of defensive cooperation. The players must converse with one another and help each other by talking and switching, in order to get to the offense and apply defensive pressure immediately. If the defense should later move into the normal defense down court when the pressure has been released and the regular defensive assignments should be desired, the switch can be made at the earliest convenience.

If pressure is being applied and the defensive player should make a mistake and let an offensive player get around him, he should immediately sprint straight for the opponents' basket and then pick up the nearest offensive player. In using the pressing defense the players must realize that many shifting combinations are possible. They should always shift to the most likely scoring threat—plugging the middle —with the free defensive player always picking up the offensive player farthest away from the basket, or the one that is the least scoring threat. This is usually the player nearest to him as he sprints down the court. By shifting in this manner the defense will not give away the cheap basket.

Basic fundamental ideas should be stressed constantly while using the pressing defenses. They are as follows:

1. Never reach for the ball.
2. Always be ready to move back on defense.
3. Keep pressure on the player with the ball at all times.
4. Remember that the idea is not to take the ball away from the opponents, but rather to harass them to such an extent that they are forced into a mistake. This can be just any mistake that will give possession of the ball to the defense.
5. The defense should always remember that the first job is to stop the dribbler—then play him tight, forcing him to get rid of the ball.
6. When defensive teammates are pressuring at the point of the ball, the defense should be alert for interceptions and for opportunities to take advantage of mistakes that the ball handler might make.
7. The players should play defense constantly. They should not wait until their offensive opponent secures the ball to start defensive play. They should play their man through the ball, and anticipate what the player with the ball is going to do. By anticipating his move the defensive player can gain the needed advantage.
8. There are three things every player should always keep in mind—the player he is guarding, the ball, and his responsibility of sagging into the middle to help a teammate who has been caught by making an error.

9. All players should be ready to stop the immediate scoring threat at any time.

REASONS FOR USING A FULL-COURT PRESS

It has been said that possession of the ball is the best defense. This is very true, and this is the best reason for using any pressure type defense. When possession of the ball is lost, one of the best ways of getting it back is by superb defensive play. Today, the rules of the game cause the offensive team to give up possession of the ball every time they score. The pressing defenses, when executed properly, can assure a quicker return to ball possession. By pressing, by harassing, and by worrying the opponents at every opportunity, the defense can force them into mistakes that will give them that coveted ball possession—that thing without which they cannot score.

By pressing, the defense can force their opponents to play into their hands and provide opportunities for interceptions. All this can be done without excessive fouling if the defense has the proper attitude and a thorough knowledge of the defensive fundamentals of the game. Proper attitudes and knowledge can be developed by working on body balance, good footwork, quickness, and alertness.

There is one other thing to remember about pressure defenses. A pressing team will get by with committing many fouls during a game. The officials do not like to call fouls constantly. They may start calling them close early in the game, but soon the officials start thinking, "I can't be blowing this whistle all the time." The result is that they loosen up and stop calling the fouls. As a result the pressing aggressive team gets by with committing many fouls during the course of a game.

Other and more specific reasons for using the press are as follows:

1. During the early season games, the opponents will not be prepared to handle the press.
2. It will speed up the tempo of the slow break, or set attack team, and cause them to be forced out of their style of play and to make more errors.
3. The pressing defense can be used to outlast a team that is in poor physical condition.
4. The team *must* use the press when behind and in the late stages of the ball game. It is not pessimistic to be prepared for being

behind in the score—something that is bound to happen.

5. It is an aggressive defense, and it is a good one to use when players are keyed up. The aggressiveness of the defense also carries over into the offensive play—resulting in a more aggressive game.

6. It is a good defense to use in an important or key ball game, such as a championship game where it it is a good idea to press in the first four or five minutes. This is the time the opponents may be determined not to make a mistake. By forcing them into an early mistake, it could upset them, and provide the margin of victory at the very onset of the game. Being tense and determined not to make a mistake causes a team to be more susceptible to defensive pressure.

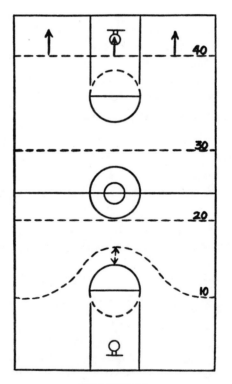

DIAGRAM 5-1

7. The pressing defense will tend to loosen the players up and cause them to play a more relaxed game.

8. Sometime during the first half of the game, other things being equal, a press should be applied to test the opponents just to see if they can handle the pressure. For example, mid-way in the first half of a college game, or early in the second quarter of a high school game is a good time to use this type of defense. This can provide the information needed and give the telltale signals as to how to proceed during the second half, determining late game strategies.

9. It is also a good idea and very effective to use a full-court press for six or seven minutes, then use a half-court press, alternating the attacks. Alternating the 20, 30 and 40 defenses, along with dropping into the hole with the 10 defense at times, can be very effective.

DIAGRAM 5-1—This diagram shows the points or areas where the pressure is to be applied in the 40 defense. The defensive contact should be made as quickly as possible and at a point somewhere beyond the front-court free-throw line area, and from there to the front-court end-line. The pressure should be applied immediately and be instantaneous. It should be applied at an appropriate and convenient time such as following a score by a basket, or a free throw, or the awarding of the ball to the opponent out of bounds in this area for any other reason.

DIAGRAM 5-2—This diagram shows pressure being applied to the player taking the ball out of bounds. X1 should pressure 01 in every way possible—trying to get him to throw a lob pass, a high long pass, or a bounce pass. His hands and arms should be flailing and especially working at head and shoulder level to encourage the offensive player to make the type of pass desired. The use of the voice, and other disconcerting efforts should be encouraged by the defense. X2, X3, X4, and X5 should play an overshift toward the ball side on defense, and work for pass interceptions. The farther the opponent is from the ball, the farther the defensive player can play from them and still maintain good defensive position. Their position and play will still be determined and be relative to two imaginary lines—one from the opponent to his basket, and the other from the opponent to the ball. Any adjustments must be relative to these two lines, and the defensive position will be adjusted according to the opponent's distance from the ball and the basket.

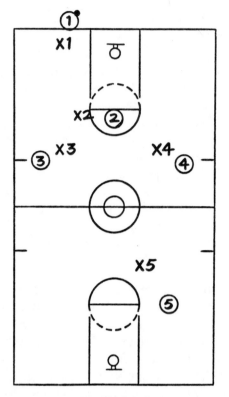

DIAGRAM 5-2

DIAGRAM 5-3—Should X1 decide to take the option that calls for two-timing the possible pass receiver on the inbounds pass-in, he would play as shown in this diagram. No harassment is to be put on 01. He is free to pass the ball inbounds without interference. He does have the five-second time limit of the rule, of course. X1 teams up with X2 to make it difficult for 02 to receive the ball. If 03 should break up the court to receive the pass, X1 can direct his energies to help X3. 04 might also break up court. Actually X1 and X2 should strongly zone the area to momentarily help on two-timing the most likely receiver of the inbounds pass-in from 01, with the expectation of making an interception. By using this tactic, it is hoped that 01 will throw a long pass that can be intercepted.

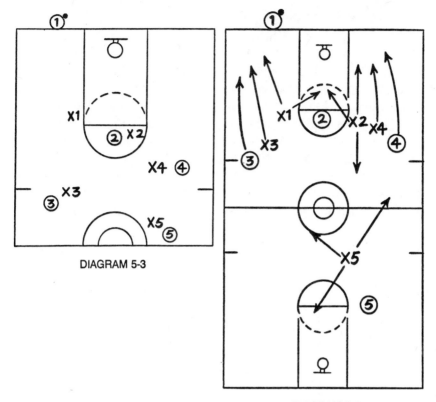

DIAGRAM 5-3

DIAGRAM 5-4

DIAGRAM 5-4—This diagram shows how X1 and X2 strongly zone the area of the possible pass-in from 01. This is applying the ideas given in Diagram 5-3 further. X1 and X2 should two-time 02. X1 should team up with X3 in guarding 03, while X2 can team up with X4 in guarding 04. As soon as the ball is passed inbounds, and 01 enters the court, X1 must be ready to do a release and make sure that 01 is guarded. It should be noted that with 05 playing deep down court, X5 can play some distance from him toward the ball. X5 can move faster than a long pass being made down court to 05, and could intercept long passes to the middle court or back court areas. He should also be responsible for the area behind him toward the basket. He must prevent the cheap basket, should the offense move down court quickly.

DIAGRAM 5-5—When using the 40 defense, many situations will arise whereby the players can help each other. The defensive players should learn to work together in these situations. They can do this by constantly talking and communicating with each other. In this diagram, X1 loses his opponent 01 down court and gets behind him on a driving dribble down the floor. To rectify this situation, X1 immediately *sprints* straight for the opponent's basket. X3, X4, and X5 drop off to help X1, and to plug the middle. X2 should sprint back until he is as deep as the ball. X3 steps out to stop the dribbler. If 03 has not been an aggressive mover, X1 can shift to him. Several defensive combinations can be possible as a result of this kind of a situation. Note that X4 and X5 will be dropping off to prevent the offense from obtaining the cheap basket.

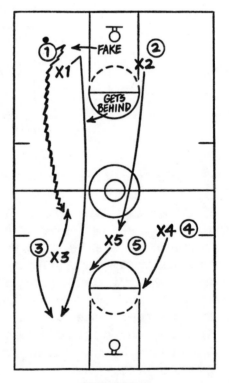

DIAGRAM 5-5

DIAGRAM 5-6—In the previous situation described in Diagram 5-5, this help situation could be possible, although it is somewhat extreme. As shown in this diagram, when X1 gets behind his opponent 01 moving down court, X3, X4, and X5 drop off to zone the area until the situation is resolved. X4 starts out tight and high in guarding 04, but knowing his responsibilities to guard the rear and the area behind him near the basket, he drops back and toward the middle of the court. With 03 cutting deep, X4 picks him up. At the same time, X5 will now shift to 04 with X1 sliding onto 05. X2, sprinting back as deep as the ball, is also back in the area to help as X3 steps out to stop 01. X5 could have dropped back to pick up 03, with X4 sliding onto 05. Now X1 could pick up 04, or work out a sliding combination with X2—one taking 04, and the other 02. This way the defense stops the immediate threat. A change back to assignments can be made as soon as it is convenient.

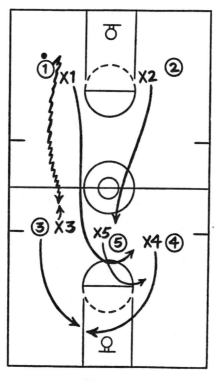

DIAGRAM 5-6

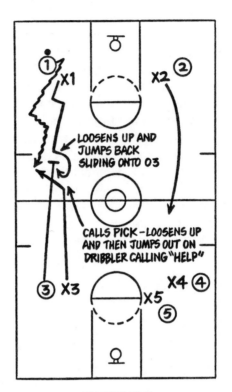

DIAGRAM 5-7

DIAGRAM 5-7—When using the man-to-man pressing defense, the defense must be constantly alert for a pick from the rear. The situation calls for quick thinking and a high degree of teamwork between the defensive players involved. The back defensive player should be responsible for the talking, and for warning the defensive player who is about to be screened from behind. Every defensive man is responsible for knowing what the situation is behind him. The pick can be avoided by using a "help" situation as previously described. The back player calls "pick" as early as possible. When the defensive player guarding the dribbler hears this, he immediately loosens up by jumping back and out of the play. The back defensive player jumps out to take the dribbler, and the defensive player about to be picked shifts right onto the offensive player who was attempting to pick. As shown in this diagram, X3 calls "pick" and immediately switches to 01. At the same time, X1 jumps back out of the pick and immediately shifts onto 03. Should 03 roll out on a cut toward the basket, X1 should sprint toward the basket to head him off. X5 and X4 should loosen up to help.

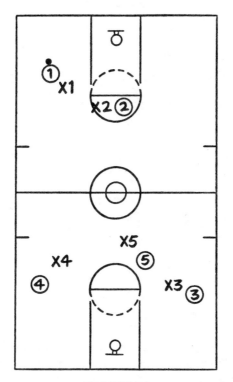

DIAGRAM 5-8

DIAGRAM 5-8—In the 40 press, the defense will overplay the offense when the ball is situated in the back court. The farther away the ball is, the more the defense overplays the offense. The distance the defense will overplay will be determined not only by the position of the ball and the opponent, but their own speed, and the speed of their opponent. They must read their opponent, understand what he can or might do, and also play the ball through their opponent. They must read the actions and intentions of the ball handler, and anticipate what he is going to do, so they can be ready to react to any situation that might develop.

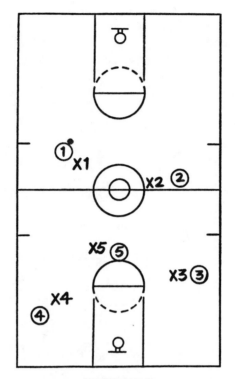

DIAGRAM 5-9

DIAGRAM 5-9—As the ball is advanced down the court, and the distance between the ball and the opponent is shortened, the defense will need to change positions accordingly, as shown in this diagram. When playing defense in these situations, the defensive player should not play close to the opponent. The defense should be instructed to keep away from the offensive player and not be fooled by his fakes. The general movements of the offensive player should be watched by the defensive player, and he should be guarded according to the position of the ball. In reverse of this, the player should, when on offense against this type of defense, get in close to the defensive player, crowd him, get him moving with him, and then move out to meet the ball.

DIAGRAM 5-10—This diagram shows how, in a different situation, the defensive players should react if an offensive player should break free

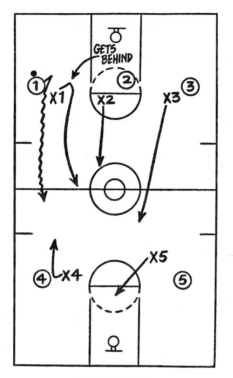

DIAGRAM 5-10

deep down court. The entire defensive team must leave their opponents, sprint toward the opponents' basket, and pull into the middle to plug it and stop the immediate scoring threat. X1 should sprint back and the situation should be maneuvered by switching and shifting to stop the loose offensive player with the ball. Pressure should be kept on the ball handler at all times. Everybody should help the defensive player guarding the man with the ball.

APPLYING THE OVERSHIFT PRINCIPLE TO THE 40 DEFENSE

In the 40 defense the standard procedure under ordinary circumstances is to apply the "20 Principle" using an overshift. The defense should force the offensive players to the outside and toward the sidelines. This maneuver forces the offensive players to take longer routes to the offensive basket, and as a result enables the defense to use the sidelines and trap areas more advantageously. By keeping the offensive player to the outside of the court it also enables the defense to pursue a shorter path to the middle of the court in their recovery attempts when the offense outmaneuvers them in down court areas.

If scouting reports or player weaknesses of opponents indicate that it would be best to do so, the 40 defense can be applied with the "10 Principle" in the overshift. In this situation, the defense would force the offensive players to the middle of the court areas so as to secure two-timing situations, and to exploit any weakness the offense might have in this respect. At times the defense should try both methods to find which one works to the best advantage.

SECTION TWO

The Great Zone Defenses

6

THE NUMBER 11 DEFENSE:
The Bottle Defense

Up to this point, the defenses presented as a part of *Basketball's Ten Greatest Defenses* have all been man-to-man defenses. The defenses presented have been applications of the basic defensive concepts presented in chapter 1. This chapter, plus the next two chapters will present and explain the three basic zone defenses used and applied in the 10 defensive area. Remember that in this defensive system, any defense numbered less than 20 will be a defense applied to the 10 defensive area or, as illustrated, to the area within a normal offensive scoring range. Later chapters will present the half-court, three-fourths-court, and the full-court zone pressing defenses.

It has been previously explained that a man-to-man defense in this system uses and applies zone principles. Likewise any zone defense in the system will use and apply man-to-man principles. In reality, all defenses used will be combination defenses, applying the strong points of both the man-to-man and the zone defense as much as possible.

The number 11 defense explained and illustrated in this chapter is a 1-2-2 zone defense. It is sometimes called the "bottle" or the "jug" defense. The shifts of the defense are fairly simple. It can be put into effect very easily and give the impression to the opposition that they face an entirely new defense, when in actuality, it may differ very little from the previous defense being used. Some offenses use a box formation with one player bringing the ball up to the front court attack. The 11 defense (1-2-2 zone) gives a perfect match-up against such an offensive formation, and it can sometimes be used without the offensive team realizing that a switch in defenses has been made.

Before giving the details of the shifts in the number 11 defense, some statements concerning facts and principles common to all zone defenses will be made. Zone defenses have long been a part of defensive basketball. Low ceilings and narrow courts were among the first reasons for deserting man-to-man and going to zone defenses. With the standardization of courts, and increased range and accuracy in the shooting ability of the players, zones declined for a time. Then came the 3-second rule, the 12-foot lane, and strong screening games —factors that caused the resurgence of the zone defenses. There is a feeling that any time a team cannot cope with the screening game, or when they are in foul trouble, they must go to a zone defense. These are good reasons for using a zone defense. Certainly every team must have a zone defense, or defenses, as a part of their defensive repertoire. Zone defenses can give the team a needed change of pace. The zone at times can be orchestrated to the best use of team personnel. It can give a change of pace, rest the personnel, help if in foul trouble, and give the help needed in many special situations that come up in a game and during the season.

ZONE DEFENSE PRINCIPLES

There are certain zone principles that apply to the use of all zone defenses.

1. When the defensive player finds a man with the ball in his area, he should press *him* with aggressiveness, and ignore other offensive players in his area.
2. When the defensive player finds no one in his zone, he should find the area that has more than one opponent in it, and move in to pick up the extra man.
3. When the defensive player finds more than one man in his zone area, and none of them have the ball, he should play the opponent nearest the ball.
4. The defensive player should never, under any circumstance, allow a man to drive around him.
5. When in a zone defense, the defensive players should keep the hands and arms at least shoulder high.
6. The defensive player should not try to steal the ball on the dribble, but should concentrate on position, stance, and sound defensive maneuvers.

7. When guarding a dribbler, the defensive player should stick with him if he dribbles from one zone to another, unless he can be shifted to a defensive teammate in that area without difficulty.
8. After a shot, the defensive player should always block out the man in his area, and then go for the ball.
9. The defense should talk—talk to teammates, letting them know what is happening in their area.
10. While the zone defensive concept is to concentrate upon the ball, and to keep all eyes on the man with the ball, the defensive players must still be aware of the position of opponents with respect to the ball and their own zone area of coverage. To this extent, they must be *mannish*.
11. The defensive players must play together as a completely coordinated unit, making their shifts in complete unison, if they are to keep all the areas covered and the shooting lanes blocked.

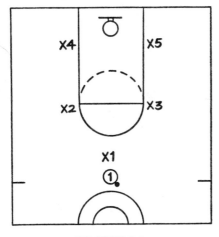

DIAGRAM 6-1

DIAGRAM 6-1—In the 11 defense, the players line up in a 1-2-2 zone defense, as shown in this diagram, when the ball is out in front at the position held by 01. The defense has weaknesses in the middle, and pernaps on the·side. However, the defense allows certain players to be kept in advantageous rebounding areas. It can give good match-up possibilities. It is also a very flexible defense, and can be varied as needed to utilize players in the various areas.

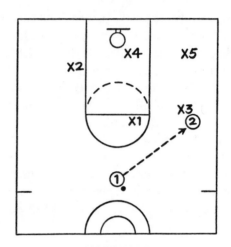

DIAGRAM 6-2

DIAGRAM 6-3

DIAGRAM 6-2—If the ball is passed from 01 to 03, the defense shifts as shown in this diagram. Note the position of X2. He should be one of the best rebounders, since most offensive teams attack a zone defense to the right side of the floor. The positions of X2 and X4 may be interchanged to take advantage of player strengths, as will be shown in later diagrams.

DIAGRAM 6-3—When the ball is passed from 03 to 05 as shown in this diagram, the players shift as shown. Note the rebounding positions of X2 and X1. Also note that after the first pass, the defense in effect becomes a 2-3 zone.

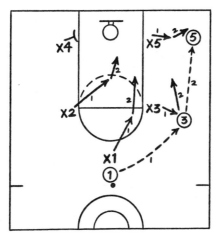

DIAGRAM 6-4

DIAGRAM 6-4—The defense may be fluctuated or varied in the shifts if it is desired to keep X4 in a more advantageous rebounding position. This is shown in this diagram. When the ball is passed from 01 to 03, to 05, the defensive players shift as indicated. X2 shifts into the middle position on the back line, and X4 holds his position to be able to have a better rebounding position on the side of the basket away from the ball. If the ball goes to the left side, the shifts would be the same in reverse, to the other side. The shifts of X2 and X4 have been changed from those shown in the previous three diagrams to show the variation possible in the shifts to take advantage of personnel.

DIAGRAM 6-5—If the ball should be passed from 03 to 05 as shown in this diagram, the defensive players X5 and X4 are both in position to harass him. They move immediately to attack him. The other players have very little moves to make, but must be aware of the positions and movements of the opponents.

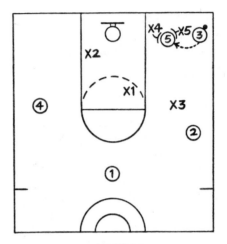

DIAGRAM 6-5

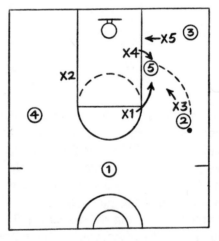

DIAGRAM 6-6

DIAGRAM 6-6—The pivot-post player should be covered as shown in this diagram. When 05, the pivot-post player, moves into the area, with the ball at 02, X1 and X4 should be aware of his move and vary their shifts so as to be able to help out and attack him if 02 should pass to him. X4 takes a good position behind 05. X1 should front 05 to prevent passes to him, if possible.

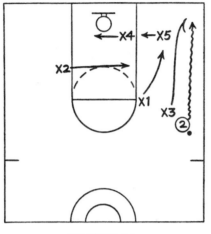

DIAGRAM 6-7

DIAGRAM 6-7—If the ball is at the position shown in this diagram, and 02 should dribble to the corner, X3 should take him man-to-man. This applies anytime a wingman dribbles to the corner. When this happens, X1 takes the position ordinarily held by X3, had the ball been passed to that position. X2 shifts in behind X1, and X4 covers the basket area opposite the ball, with X5 taking the lane area on the side of the ball.

The 11 defense gives a good change of pace, utilizes all the rebound possibilities, and can give the team good opportunities for fast break possibilities—all reasons why the team may want to shift to, and use this defense.

7

THE NUMBER 12 DEFENSE:
The 2-3 Zone

The number 12 defense is a 2-3 zone defense, applied in the 10 defensive area. It is probably the most commonly used zone defense. It gives good defensive rebounding positions in the area near the basket. It also provides an excellent base from which the fast break attack may be launched. It is weak in the side area around the free throw line extended. The principles for zone defenses given in chapter 6 apply to this defense as well, and will not be repeated here.

The 2-3 zone and the 2-1-2 zone defenses very closely resemble each other, and at times function in the same manner. The deployment of the middle man in his defensive shifts is the only difference between the two defenses. When the middle man plays higher and is expected to do a wider coverage in the side areas, the defense could be called a 2-1-2 zone defense. For purposes of defenses in this book, the 2-3 and the 2-1-2 zones will be regarded as the same and called the number 12 defense.

The 12 defense is an excellent defense to use when the opponents have two fine guards that do the major part of the scoring. The two front line defensive men can pick up these guards tight and play aggressively on them, knowing that the back line of the zone defense can give them help when outmaneuvered. This defense will work well against the offense that features a strong pivot-post player.

In this case, the middle man on the defensive back line can play the pivot player man-to-man, fronting him and playing him tight as long as he is in the defensive area A (pivot-post area). The 12 defense will also function well against offenses that use guard-forward interchange and weave movements.

DIAGRAM 7-1—This diagram shows the principal coverage areas for each defensive position. The position of X5 will vary the most in coverage from one system to another, and from coach to coach. If X5, the middle player on the back line of the defense, is given a wider coverage and is expected to move out to cover the flank areas on the side, the defense will be more like a 2-1-2 zone. If the players in the positions of X4 and X3 are to make this coverage, then the shift of X5 must be somewhat different, as will be shown. Actually, in most situations, X5 will be expected to do a strong coverage in the pivot-post defensive area (area A) to prevent a weakness in front of the basket, while X3 and X4 can move out to protect the sides to a point just back of the free throw line extended. If there is a need for the shift to be otherwise, the adjustment can easily be made. That is why the 2-3 zone and the 2-1-2 zone defenses are practically the same, and are treated as such, here in the 12 defense.

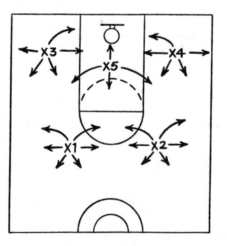

DIAGRAM 7-1

DIAGRAM 7-2—If the ball should be brought up the floor by 01 as shown in this diagram, on the right side of the floor, X2 would move out to take him when he comes within scoring range. X1 fills in behind X2, and X5 shifts to be in line with the position of the ball, and to possibly front any player in the pivot-post area. X3 and X4 shift as shown.

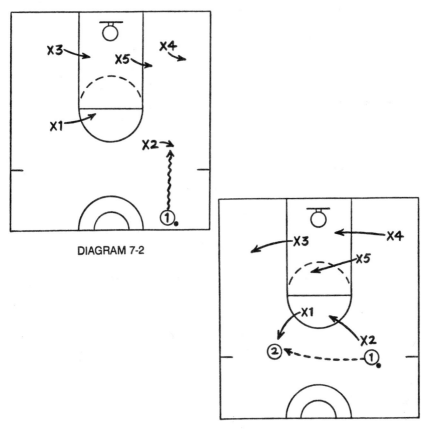

DIAGRAM 7-2

DIAGRAM 7-3

DIAGRAM 7-3—Should 01 pass the ball across court to 02 as shown in this diagram, then X1 and X2 shift positions as indicated. They make this play very much as they would in the number 10 defense, or as it would be done in a regular man-to-man defense. X5, X3, and X4 shift as shown.

DIAGRAM 7-4—If 01 should pass the ball to 03 as shown in this diagram, X4 moves out to take 03 as indicated. X5 must stay in the pivot-post area to guard 05. The other players shift as shown. In some instances, this coverage on 03 could be delegated to X5, but this could be done only when there is less pressure in the middle. If X5 should move out to the wing position to guard 03 when the ball is passed to him as shown in this diagram, the defense would be doing the shifts that are more related to a 2-1-2 zone defense.

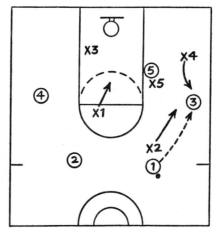

DIAGRAM 7-4

DIAGRAM 7-5—As shown in this diagram, X5 must relate his position to the position of 05. X1 must also relate his position to 02 and possibly even to 04. X3 must also relate his shift to the position of 04. A quick pass from 01 to 04 could bring problems in this situation. Note that X5 is playing very close to an imaginary line from the ball to 05. Relating their zone positions to the positions of the opponents makes the defense *mannish*.

DIAGRAM 7-6—If 03 should pass the ball to 05 at the position shown in this diagram, X5 would take 05 to the corner, and X4 would fill in behind him as shown. This would be a normal coverage position for X4, but a particular move such as this one would necessitate X5 taking 05 to the corner. The other players shift as shown.

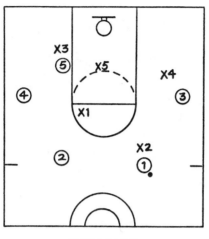

DIAGRAM 7-5

DIAGRAM 7-6

DIAGRAM 7-7—If 03 should dribble from the position shown in this diagram to the corner, X4 would take him man-to-man. X5 would shift to fill in behind him, and the other players shift as shown.

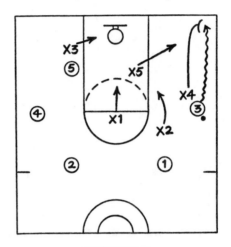

DIAGRAM 7-7

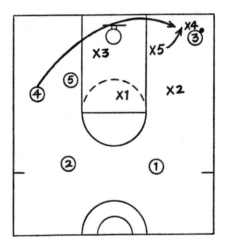

DIAGRAM 7-8

DIAGRAM 7-8—With the ball in the corner at the position shown in this diagram and in possession of 03, should either 04 or 05, or any other player move to the position shown, X5 should move to front him to prevent a pass from being made to that position or into the area.

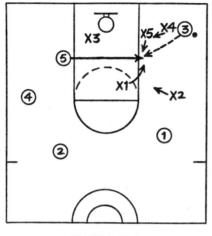

DIAGRAM 7-9

DIAGRAM 7-9—If 05 should move into the pivot-post area to receive a pass from 03, as shown in this diagram, then X5 and X1 attack him as indicated. If possible, X1 and X5 should team up to prevent the pass being made into the area. By playing his position somewhat with respect to the position of the opponent, in this case 05, X5 should be able to check and front the area enough to prevent the pass. If it does get through, he should have the help of X1 and possibly X2.

DIAGRAM 7-10—To begin their positions, X3 and X4 start as near to the free throw lane as possible. If there are no opponents behind them near the basket, they play as high as possible. If 01 or any opponent should bring the ball straight down the middle, directly to the front of the basket, X1 and X2 pinch in to prevent him from having a good passing area into the middle. They move in to close the lanes as shown in the diagram.

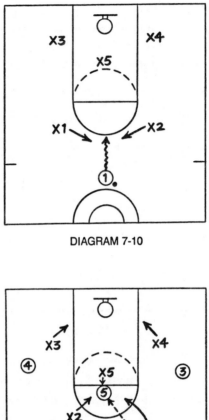

DIAGRAM 7-10

DIAGRAM 7-11

DIAGRAM 7-11—If the ball should be passed from 01 into the pivot-post position to 05 as shown in this diagram, then X2 and X1 should shift in to help X5 pressure 05. X4 and X3 should drop back toward the lane and to the rear some to protect the area. If the ball should be passed from 05 to one of the wing positions they must move out quickly to protect—but at the same time they must always be ready to help out behind the high post and to protect the baseline. Stopping the pivot-post player and play in the middle area (area A) is usually the most important play for the defensive team.

The 12 defense is a good zone defense. It is especially strong around the basket area. It gives good defense against super-scoring guards. It also furnishes a good base from which to launch a fast break attack. It can furnish the change of pace and defensive measures necessary to confound and confuse the opponents.

THE NUMBER 13 DEFENSE:
The 1-3-1 Zone

The number 13 defense is a 1-3-1 zone applied by the defense in the 10 defensive area. It is the third zone formation to be used in the defensive system explained in this book. It is a defense that should have a definite place in every defensive system because of the special strengths that it gives, and the special applications that can be made through its use.

For a time coaches were attacking all zone defenses with a 1-3-1 offensive formation. The answer to the 1-3-1 offensive formation was the 1-3-1 zone defense. It evolved as a zone match-up defense to oppose the 1-3-1 offense. It also presents special strength down through the middle in the pivot-post operational areas. It has been used consistently to stop teams that present special scoring problems from that area. It also gives good strength in the wing positions. It is weak in the corners on each side of the basket laterally to the right and left along the baseline. Not every opponent can score well from this area anyway. The strengths and weaknesses of the defense can clue the defensive team as to when to apply and use this defense. It is always one that can be used for variation of defensive patterns to surprise and confuse the offensive opponent by requiring them to make constant adjustments. If the defense is using zone formations against the opponents, it is a good idea to vary the formations to befuddle the opponents. The offense may be so occupied with making adjustments to changing defenses that they get little else accomplished.

DIAGRAM 8-1—The basic lineup of the 13 (1-3-1) defense is as shown in this diagram. X1 sets up about one step ahead of the free throw circle. X2 is on the free throw line. X4 and X5 take positions just ahead of the free throw line extended, and originally just about two strides away from the lane. X3 plays just in front of the basket.

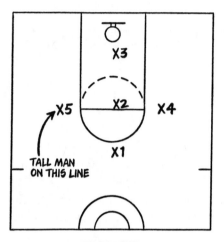

DIAGRAM 8-1

X1 must be fast, aggressive, a hustler, and perhaps the best defensive player, plus being a good leader. X4 and X5, the wing players, should be the positions for the slowest moving players, and perhaps the tallest and best rebounders. They will have less distance to transverse on the shifts, and will shift into the most favorable rebound positions as the ball is moved around by the offense in an attempt to penetrate the defense.

The player in the X2 position should be the second best defensive player, or at least the best defensive player among the taller team members. He has some moves to make on the shifts that require more distance and quick movements.

The player in the X3 position should be the fastest moving forward. His moves call for quick shifts along the baseline toward the corners. He will also be in position for some good rebounding. He may be expected to cover both corners on the defensive shift, but this responsibility could be rotated with X2. If this should be done, X3 would take the ball in the right corner, and X2 would take the left corner, with X3 dropping behind him. The diagrams that follow will show the shifts.

One of the fundamental concepts upon which the 13 defense operates is that of keeping three players between the ball and the basket at all times. Every time the ball is passed or moved, the defensive players shift so that there is always a three-player alignment present between the ball and the basket. The strength of this 1-3-1 zone defense lies in the fact that this "three players between the ball and the basket" is in effect at all times.

DIAGRAM 8-2—If the ball is passed from 01 to 02 as shown in this diagram, the defense shifts as indicated. X1 acts as a chaser out in front. In some situations he can be released to help X4 double team players in the area shown. This has to be dictated by the opposition, the talents of X1, and the particular situation. This defense can go for traps in certain areas. Each player will have basic shifts to make according to the movements of the ball. These shifts should be practiced until they become automatic with the players. Note that with 02 in possession of the ball, X4, X2, and X3 are in reality between the ball and the basket.

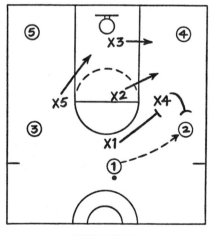

DIAGRAM 8-2

Also note that X3 cheats a little in his position toward the corner so that if the ball is passed to 04, he can move on him quickly.

DIAGRAM 8-3—When the ball is passed from 02 to 04 as shown in this diagram, the defense shifts as indicated. X3 moves out to cover the player with the ball. X2 drops in behind X3 and X5 covers the area to the left of the basket, with X1 and X4 shifting as shown. If X4 should release and go to help X3 in a double-teaming maneuver on 04, then X1 will have to float more, and be ready to cover more passing lanes, and to anticipate 04's pass. Every effort should be made to make 04 throw a long pass back out to the outside.

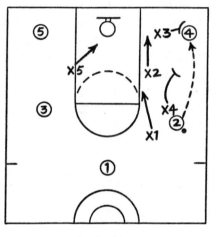

DIAGRAM 8-3

DIAGRAM 8-4—X1 chases the ball in front. If the chase leads near the defensive area of the wing men, they team up with X1. As shown in this diagram, X1 and X5 stop 01. When 01 passes off to 05 in the corner, the defense shifts as indicated.

DIAGRAM 8-5—With the ball passed to the left as shown in this diagram, the players shift as indicated. Note the three men between the ball and the basket.

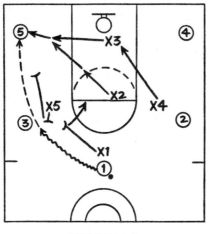

DIAGRAM 8-4

DIAGRAM 8-5

DIAGRAM 8-6—A basic difference that could be made in the shifts from the right side to the left side is shown in this diagram. On the left side, when the ball is passed from 03 to 05 in the left corner, X2 could shift to cover the corner man. This would relieve X3 of covering both corners. It

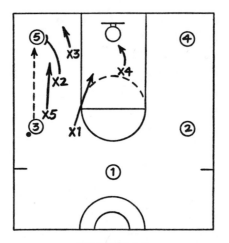

DIAGRAM 8-6

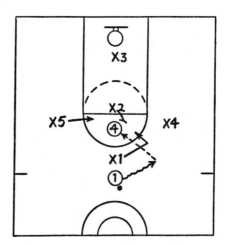

DIAGRAM 8-7

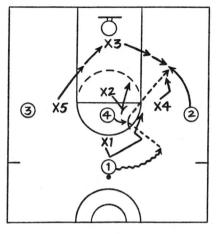

DIAGRAM 8-8

would be understood that X3 would cover the ball in the right corner, and X2 would cover the left corner, as indicated here. In this case, with the ball at the 03 position, X2 would cheat on his move to be able to move out quickly on 05 when the ball is passed to him. Now X3 drops in behind X2. X4 covers the rebound area to the right of the basket, and X5 and X1 shift as shown. Again, if X2 chases 05 toward X5, and they effect a two-timing trap, X1 must float to cover the lanes to the inside area. This difference in the shifting of the players from the right side to the left side is an optional move. If X3 can make these moves effectively, it might be best to always have X2 fall in behind X3 on these shifts, always being the middle man. However, this wide coverage could tire X3, and might be used to an advantage in some situations.

DIAGRAM 8-7—In a movement such as is shown in this diagram, with 01 passing the ball to 04 in a high post position, the defense is in a position of strength. X2, X5, and X4, and even X1 can converge on the pivot-post player as needed. These players must be careful, however, not to leave the defense weakened in the wing positions and underneath on each side of the basket. Here in the situation shown, X2 and X1 could combine harassing moves on 04, with X5 and X4 floating to cover the wing positions, and underneath to help X3, in accordance with the positions of the opponents on offense.

DIAGRAM 8-8—In an offensive move such as the one shown in this diagram, certainly X4 and X5 must be alert to the position of opponents in the wing positions who might drop suddenly deeper and pose an overload in X3's area. Here 01 passes to 04 on the pivot-post, who in turn drops the ball down on the right side to 02 cutting down from the wing. This would call for a quick move by X3 and X4. X4 must be aware of 02's movements and he can either cut off the passing lane, or help X3 double team 02 after he gets the ball. The other defensive players shift as shown.

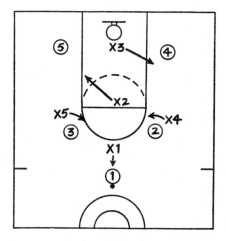

DIAGRAM 8-9

DIAGRAM 8-9—Certain offensive formations can cause this defense difficulties. As stated previously, the defense is weak along the base line on both sides of the basket to the corners. If the offense should go into the formation shown in this diagram, the defense will have to make adjustments to counter the positions of the opponents. In this offensive formation, a quick pass from 01, 02, or 03 made to 04 or 05 could cause a problem for X3. X4 and X5 should make adjustments on 02 and 03. X2 can drop back toward the baseline and cheat in a movement toward 05, while X3 makes an adjustment on 04. In actuality, X2 and X3 should float the areas, with the other defensive players becoming more *mannish* until the direction and movement of the ball is established.

DIAGRAM 8-10—The 13 defense, being a one-man front defense, will sometimes have trouble with two guards bringing the ball up as shown in this diagram. With ball movement back and forth across the front area as indicated, and with players 04, 05, and 03 in what might be termed "hard to cover positions," it sometimes makes it possible for one of the guards to deliver the ball inside to vulnerable positions. The answer is defensive adjustment to fit the situation. As shown here, 01 gets X1 declared to the right, then flips the ball back to 02, who is in a good position at the top of the circle to either shoot, or possibly pass inside to 04, or even to 03. X4 should drop down to cover the passing lanes to 05. X5 must guard 04. X3 must cheat his position toward 03. X2 can move up to give help to X1, if the offensive move proves to be damaging to the defense. If there is no effective shooter from the circle area, X2 can help X5 and X4 in two-timing players in that area.

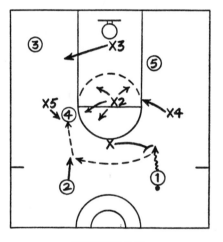

DIAGRAM 8-10

9

THE NUMBER 31 DEFENSE:
A Special Trap

The 31 defense is a special trap defense applied at the 30 defense point of contact. Just as in the 30 defense, the pressure is applied about three full strides in advance of the 10-second court division line, when the offense brings the ball up court. It starts out appearing to be a normal 30 press, but suddenly makes a two-timing, or double-teaming maneuver that requires the application of strong zone principles, with a risk element involved. It is a gamble in that it momentarily, at least, leaves the opponent farthest from the ball open. This possibly invites the long pass with hopes of interception. If the interception is not accomplished, the defense should have time enough to fill in, plug the middle, and prevent the cheap basket.

DIAGRAM 9-1—At this point the defense appears to be a normal 30 pressure defense. 01 and 02 bringing the ball up court are about to be pressured at the normal 30 defense contact point. Remember that the normal situation in the 30 defense calls for the "20 principle" of over-shifting and forcing the offense toward the side line. The dotted line areas in the diagram show the vital trap areas and coffin corners that are to be brought into play to help secure the special trap situation. The next diagrams give the succeeding steps.

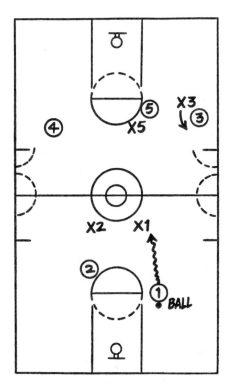

DIAGRAM 9-1

DIAGRAM 9-2—As 01 is bringing the ball up the floor, X1 steps out and forces him toward the outside and toward the corner. If 02 had the ball, X2 would make this maneuver to the opposite side of the floor and the maneuver could be worked there. Remember, in all diagrams, a maneuver shown on one side of the floor will work just the same to the opposite side. Both will not be shown here. Having forced the dribbler to the outside, X1's next maneuver is to drive him to one of the corners and stop him—to get him to pick up the ball and thus end the dribble. If at all possible, X1 must stop 01 in the corner just before he crosses the court division line. However, should he fail in this, the corner area just across the division line can also be an effective trap. Applying the trap before the division line is crossed adds to the pressure on the 10-second count, and this can give the offense dilemma needed to make the desired pass that can be intercepted by the defense. X2 fakes as if to pressure 02, but seeing X1 having turned 01 on the dribble to the

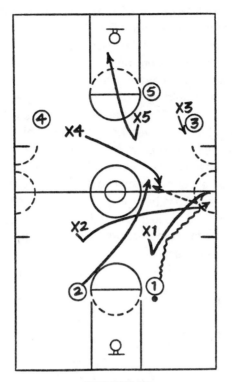

DIAGRAM 9-2

outside, and toward the corner, now completely leaves 02 open, and joins X1 in a double team trap on 01. The move is an invitation to get 01 to throw the ball to 02, or a cross court pass. After 01 had been turned toward the sideline, X4 moved farther from 04 and toward the mid-court area, and finally seeing the trap being applied on 01, he moves up fast to snag the natural pass that 01 would make to 02. The movement calls for perfect timing and teamwork. X1 must head off 01 before he can escape down the sideline. X4 must time his move properly. 04, the farthest offensive player from the ball will be left open, but in this situation, it is doubtful that 01 can successfully negotiate such a pass. X3 should play 03 tight, and X5 should play in front of 05, plus he must be ready to drop underneath the basket to protect against the cheap basket. He should also be ready to possibly move out to intercept long passes that might be made to 04. In this case, X3 protects the underbasket area, should X5 so commit himself.

DIAGRAM 9-3—In some cases, 01 will escape X1 in the first two possible corners near the court division line. If this should happen, then X3 can jump out to stop the dribbler 01, as shown in this diagram. He should try to do this just before he crosses the mid-court division line since this will keep the 5-second time limit on against the closely guarded player who is holding and/or dribbling the ball. Now X1 and X3 will double team 01. X5 will drop back to cover possible passes to 03, and X4 must drop back to cover the area behind him near the basket. X2 should now zone the mid-court area to snag interceptions, should 01 attempt to throw passes to either 04, 05, or 02 in that area. In the 31 defense, should 01 escape the first two trap areas near the division line, this one is always a possibility if 03 is playing near enough to the mid-court area for X3 to move into the play. While not as effective as the other trap, it does offer some opportunity while requiring more shifting on the part of the defense.

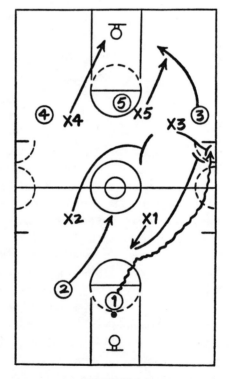

DIAGRAM 9-3

DIAGRAM 9-4—The "10 Principle" can be applied also in the 31 trap defense. Instead of forcing the dribbler to the outside, the defensive guards X1 and X2 play so as to force 01 and 02 into a cross or into the middle. They then go into a two-timing situation as shown in this diagram. X1 and X2 two-time the guard 02 who has received the ball from 01 on a cross maneuver. X1 attacks low, while X2 comes at him high, with hands up throwing a double team umbrella over 02. The back defensive men play high and for interceptions. X4 comes up fast to snag passes that might be made to 01. X5 is responsible for the area underneath the basket should an offensive breakaway come. Defensive shifting can then be made to cover the most imminent scoring threats.

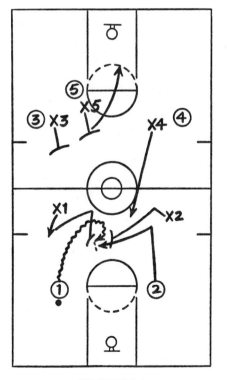

DIAGRAM 9-4

DIAGRAM 9-5—In the 31 defense, when working the "10 Principle" 01 and 02 do not have to cross for the trap to be made. If 01 can be forced into a dribble and come close to 02, the defense can jump into the trap quickly from just maneuvering the offensive players close to one another. X3, seeing this possibility, is always ready to move up to snag an interception should the dribbler throw the ball up to 02. X4 and X5 play high and tight as usual, and with play in this area X5 is responsible for the under-basket area should the offense come up with an escape.

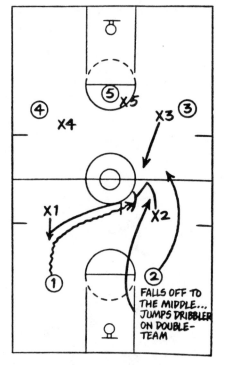

DIAGRAM 9-5

In the 31 defense there must be close cooperation between the back and front lines of defense. The back line must be ready to play high quickly, and also cover the area behind them to prevent the cheap basket when necessary. The 31 defense is a very special trap defense—and should be used only infrequently, in special situations.

If the defensive team can apply the 31 defense and effect a trap in the offensive team's back court just before they cross the division line, the defense can be very effective. Usually, as the offensive team nears the court division line, the 10-second time limit has nearly expired. For a player to now be driven to a coffin corner in the back court, or to be trapped, can cause just the reaction desired by the defense. Under the present rules in basketball, the defensive team can also have a distinct advantage even when the offensive team crosses the court division line and enters the mid-court area just beyond the division line. In the mid-court area, the offensive player is faced with a new, and a shorter time-count. A closely guarded player, while holding or dribbling the ball, or who combines holding and dribbling the ball for 5 seconds, must give up a held ball. This pressure can work effectively for the 31 defense, especially when the ball handler has been driven into one of the corners or trap areas and is double-teamed there.

10

THE NUMBER 31Z DEFENSE:
The Half-court Zone Press

The 31Z defense is another defense applied in the 30 defensive series pressure points. It is definitely a half-court to a three-fourths-court zone press defense with some *mannish* features. It lines up as a 1-2-2 zone applied at the 30 defense point of contact. It gives a change of pace to the 30 defense, and in rotation with the 30 and 31 defenses, can bring extreme pressure on the offense at the 10-second court division line. The defense should be used in two situations in particular. The first is when the half-court pressure defenses are to be applied to upset the offensive team, and the second is in situations where the offense has a lead and is using a delayed offense, or a stalling game. In this situation, the defense is applied more nearly to the 20 defensive area, but for the sake of conserving numbers, it is best to keep the numbered series the same, since the working of the defense is exactly the same in this situation.

DIAGRAM 10-1—The defense lines up as shown in this diagram. X1 is ready to attack at the 30 defensive line as the ball is brought up court. X2 and X3 wait just behind, or right at the court division line. X4 and X5 will line up at about the free throw line and circle area. If the offense has men playing deep near the basket and along the baseline, X4 and X5 will have to make adjustments in their positions to make sure that long passes cannot be heaved to players in this area. They might invite such passes, while making sure they could intercept such throws. The dotted lines give the basic coverage areas for each player at the beginning of the defense. Also keep in mind the trap areas on the court shown in

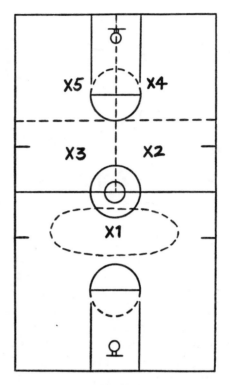

DIAGRAM 10-1

previous diagrams. The defense is *mannish* in that all the court positions are interchangeable according to the way the offensive players line up—that is, the defense will change positions in order to more nearly match the offensive players in height.

X1 should be the most active, aggressive, and the quickest defensive player. It will be his duty to turn the offense in the direction desired as it comes up the court. X2 and X3 are next in these same mental and physical qualities, and will work with X1 to secure two-timing trap situations and to make interceptions. X4 and X5 are responsible for the area near the basket. They zone their areas according to the positions of the opponents, and play for interceptions, while also protecting underneath.

DIAGRAM 10-2—In this diagram X1 has turned the dribbler 01 in the desired direction. It could be the desired direction for several

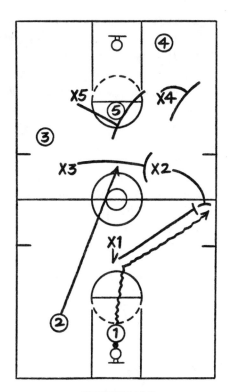

DIAGRAM 10-2

reasons—01's weakest side move or direction, or perhaps the defense desires to move him away from 03 as far as possible. If his weakest move is to his left, then X1 should move him to the left. If at all possible, X1 and X2 must secure the trap in the corner just before 01 crosses the division line. This trap applies the most pressure, and causes the greatest dilemma to the ball handler because usually he is nearing the 10-second time limit count as he nears the division line. He is more likely to throw the ball up for interception from here than from anywhere else. X3 will play the mid-court area for interceptions and will vary his position according to the opponents' positions, and will attempt to read what the ball handler will do with the ball. It calls for quick and decisive decisions on his part and at times his decisions call for a gamble that can lose. X4 and X5 zone their areas also, but make sure the area underneath the basket is protected. They will also vary their positions according to the positions of the opponents. With the double teaming operation of X1 and X2, the idea is that the defense will shift so that the man left open will be the opponent farthest from the ball. This is to invite the long pass. If an interception is not possible, the defense will still have time to shift positions and prevent the cheap basket. The offensive player forced to make a long pass will telegraph his intentions, thus making it easier for the defense to read him and anticipate his move, and to make interceptions.

DIAGRAM 10-3—If X1 and his teammate, either X2 or X3, cannot trap 01 just before he crosses the division line, the next most desirable trap area is in the corner just after crossing the division line. Here he may feel relief on evading the 10-second count, only now to find himself

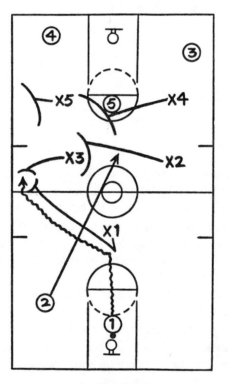

DIAGRAM 10-3

trapped and guarded with a new and shorter count—the 5-second count on a player who is closely guarded while dribbling and/or holding the ball. The count is continuous on both and he can secure no relief until he either clears the mid-court area, or he passes off to a teammate. Here X1 has turned 01 to the left, and being unable to trap him before crossing the division line, X1 and X3 succeed in stopping him just after crossing the line. Here they now have the able help of a side line and the court division line in throwing a double team umbrella over him. X2 now zones the mid-court area for interceptions while X5 and X4 zone their areas as shown, and are in good position to make interceptions on passes to 04 and 05. 03, the opponent farthest from the ball is the one the least guarded. X2, X4, and X5 must be aware of the positions of the opponents. They will vary their positions accordingly, and as to what they can read into the intent of the ball handler.

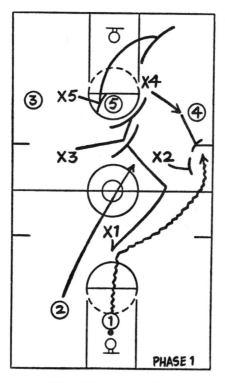

DIAGRAM 10-4—PHASE 1

DIAGRAM 10-4, Phase 1—If X1, in working with X2 and X3, cannot trap the ball handler just before crossing the court division line or right after crossing it, the next trap possibility is right at the mid-court marker line. In this diagram, X1 turned the dribbler right, but he escaped down the side line. Now X4 steps up to help, and with X2 they apply the trap right at the mid-court fore-court corner. If 04 is in the area, he could provide an outlet for 01, but the trap attempt is worth the try. When the trap is applied here, X5 moves down low as shown. X3 drops to the top of the circle area, and X1 does a release to the mid-court area to work for interceptions there. The following diagrams will show shifting patterns for the defense, when 01 succeeds in passing out of his dilemma.

DIAGRAM 10-5, Phase 2—Here in Phase 2, with the trap applied in Diagram 10-4, 01 succeeds in passing out to 04. Now X5 and X4 go for a double team on 04. X3 drops down to cover the underbasket area. X1 zones the area near the top of the circle, and X2 zones the mid-court area for interceptions. X2 will vary his position between 01 and 03 and what he can read into what the ball handler 04 will do with the ball. 02's position will also be a consideration.

DIAGRAM 10-6, Phase 3—Going back to Diagram 10-4 again, if when

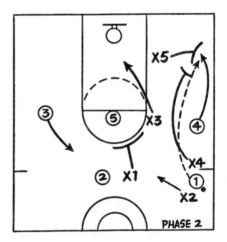

DIAGRAM 10-5—PHASE 2

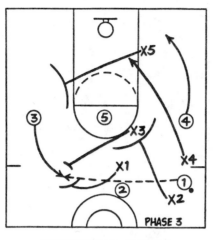

DIAGRAM 10-6—PHASE 3

01 is trapped as shown in this diagram, he should throw a pass over X1 to 03 in the mid-court area, the shifts will be as shown. X3 and X1 should double team 03. X4 should release and drop back underneath the basket area. X5 should move out to cover the top of the circle area toward the ball, while X2 should zone the mid-court area and he will vary his movements according to the positions of 01 and 02 and what he can read into the intent of the ball handler, 03.

DIAGRAM 10-7, Phase 1—Although the intent of this defense is to force the offense into errors and trap situations just before or just after they cross the 10-second court division line, if the offense comes across the line and then goes into a delayed offense or uses keep-away tactics, this defense should still be used. There are many delayed offense patterns, but this diagram shows one that is very common. When X1 forces a movement from 01 and he passes to 04 coming off a screen from near the basket area, X2 and X1 double team 04 as shown in the mid-court area. X4 adjusts out of the screen and zones his area. X5 and X3 zone the area shown and will be alert for interceptions on passes that might be made to 03, 05, or 01 as he cuts through the middle. 04 has the 5-second count on him and must move the ball.

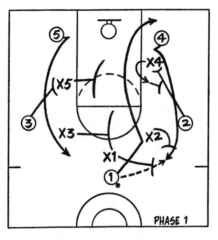

DIAGRAM 10-7—PHASE 1

DIAGRAM 10-8, Phase 2—Continuing from Diagram 10-7, if when trapped 04 selects to pass to 01 as shown here, the defense shifts as indicated. X2 and X4 double team 01. X5 moves over to zone the area vacated by X4. X3 drops back to guard underneath the basket and to zone passes to this area. X1 releases and zones the top of the circle area near the mid-court. His position will vary according to the movements of 04 and 05 and as to what he can read into the intent of the ball handler. If 04 is the most logical outlet for 01, X1 should play for such interceptions. Again, the offensive player farthest from the ball has been left open, in this case 05.

DIAGRAM 10-9, Phase 3—Back again to Diagram 10-7, if when trapped, 04 selects to pass to 05 as shown in this diagram, the defense shifts as indicated. X1 and X3 double team 05 in the mid-court area. The 5-second count is on. X5 zones the area to the left of the basket, and cuts off possible passes to 03. X4 zones the underbasket area and could intercept long passes that might be attempted to 01 and 02. X2 zones the mid-court area and his specific moves will be determined by reading the intent of 05 and the movements of 04 in the mid-court area.

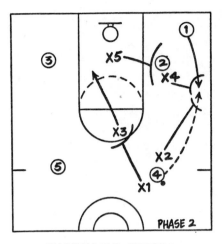

DIAGRAM 10-8—PHASE 2

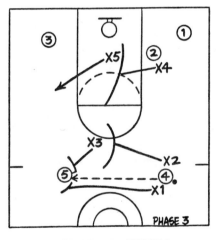

DIAGRAM 10-9—PHASE 3

The 31Z defense works continuously for trap and two-timing situations, making shifts in assignments and positions constantly, so that only the offensive player farthest from the ball will be open. It invites the long pass, and pressures for interceptions. It uses all the trap corners possible, and exploits the 10-second rule at the division line, and the 5-second rule, applicable to the mid-court area. Worked properly it can pay rich dividends for the defense by bringing about the desired turnovers by the offense.

11

THE NUMBER 41 DEFENSE:
The Full-court Zone Press

The number 41 defense is a full-court zone press. It is applied at the 40 defense pressure points. As a zone defense press, it features some *mannish* principles. The defensive alignment of positions on the court will vary somewhat according to the positions of the offensive players. This is to say that while it is a zone, the defense must be aware of where the offensive players are in the various areas, and will play accordingly. The defense lines up as a 1-2-1-1. It is called a 41 in this defensive system because of the 40 attack area, and the one-man spearheading the attack. It is also usually the first, and most used of all the full-court zone presses.

The defense concedes the first pass inbounds. At times, it also awaits for a first commitment from the offense, after which pressure is applied. At other times, the defense will move to apply pressure immediately upon the offensive player receiving the inbounds pass to get a commitment from him. After the offense is committed, the defense will go all out to intercept the second pass or to trap a player and force an offensive error. The defense will try to prevent deep, penetrating passes, and at the same time it will encourage long passes, lob passes, bounce passes, and backward passes toward their own basket. The 10-second rule is with the defense in that, once the ball is passed inbounds, the offense must make a commitment to do something toward getting the ball out of the back court and into their front court. Once a player on offense starts a dribble in his back court, the defense should stop the dribbler and try to get him to throw the ball somewhere. Two-timing or double teaming tactics should be used to accomplish this. Once the dribbler has been stopped, defensive teammates play hard for interceptions.

DIAGRAM 11-1—A normal lineup for the 41 defense is as shown in this diagram. Note that it is what would be referred to as the 1-2-1-1 alignment. It could also be called a diamond one, with X1, X2, X3, and X4 forming the diamond and X5 playing the one back position.

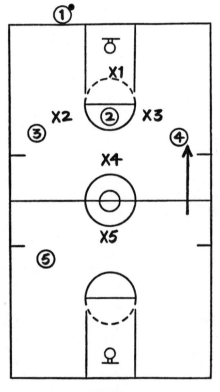

DIAGRAM 11-1

REQUISITES FOR THE PLAYER POSITIONS IN THE 41 DEFENSE

The player in the X1 position is the lead man in the defense. He should be the fastest and quickest reacting, and the player with the most persistence and endurance. If he has long arms and quick hands it will enhance his ability to play this position. Ordinarily, on most teams, this player might be the smallest, most tenacious guard, but if this player is tall, it can add to his ability to overpower the opponent in the trap. This player, as the lead man in the defense, will determine as much as possible the direction of the first pass, so he must have the ability to size up the floor situation, and be able to react accordingly in determining the direction in which he wants the first pass to go.

The players at positions X2 and X3 should have much the same as far as physical requirements are concerned. Usually one of these players will be a guard and the other a forward, but combined guard-forward qualities would be an advantage. These two players will be involved in trapping situations continuously with X1. Fast reactions, quick hands, and quick movements are assets that will enhance their play. Both X2 and X3 must have good judgment concerning the application of the trap, and know when to force opponents toward the middle, and know when to allow the play to go toward the side line and away from the middle. Actually X2 and X3 will be involved in trap situations with both X1 and X4. As will be noted in later diagrams, when the offensive player escapes down the side line away from the middle, trap situations with X4 will occur. Other trap plays involving X4 could also occur in plays away from the side line in what might be termed a deep middle position.

X4 and X5 have the most challenging positions on the floor. Both positions call for the ability to read the opponent, and to anticipate and judge where the pass is going to be made out of the trap area. X4 will be involved more in going for the second pass, or the pass that will be thrown from the trap situations set up by X1, X2, and X3. Actually X4 has the most exciting position to play and his judgment and anticipation of the opponents' moves will on many occasions be the determining factor as to whether or not the press succeeds. He must have good lateral movements to the right and left. He should be strong, tireless, and highly motivated by a situation that demands keen perception and challenge.

X5 must have the ability to react to a changing situation. He must be able to anticipate and to know when he can go for an interception. He must be able to cover the long passes made to the division line, and deeper. He must have the ability to judge when to defend the basket, and when he can leave the basket area undefended. His position is a very challenging one in that he must be able to react to mistakes made by either his teammates or the opponents. In case of a mistake by the opponents, he must be able to make the move that would cash in on it. If the mistake is one made by his teammates, he must defend the basket, and be able to hold the opponents at bay until his teammates can recover and help him. He must never allow the cheap basket.

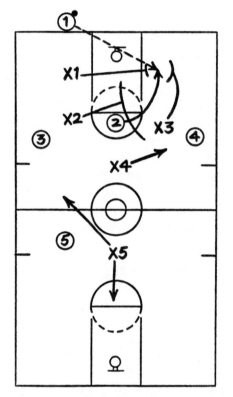

DIAGRAM 11-2

DIAGRAM 11-2—While the first pass inbounds is forfeited, and seldom contested, nevertheless, the defense does all that it can to determine the direction of the pass. By lining up as shown in this diagram, X1 encourages 01 taking the ball out of bounds to pass to the right side of the floor (defensive right). This pass made back across the court and under the basket cuts down on his passing possibilities (basket and hanging net obstructs view and cuts down area possibilities) and encourages the bounce pass to this area. Once the ball is inbound the defense shifts as shown. X3 prevents 02 from going down the outside and turns him so that X1 and X3 may double team him. X2 will cover the middle of the floor to his right and around the free throw circle area. X4 is responsible for the area back of X1 and X3 and to his right. Should the ball have gone to the other side of the floor, these shifts would just be reversed to the other side. X5 has the most challenging position and must cover long passes made to the division line or deeper. He is also responsible for the area underneath the defensive basket, and he must prevent the cheap basket. He must be unusually adept at reading the intent of the ball handler, and at reacting accordingly. X4's position is also a vital challenge, as he will be in the area of the second pass the most frequently, and must correctly read the intent of the ball handler if he is to get the necessary one step advantage that is needed to make the interception. At times, if 02 does not advance the ball immediately, X3 and X1 will advance to meet him. Usually, however, 02 will make the initial move due to the pressure of the 10-second rule, and from this thrust, X1 and X3 can make their commitment against him.

DIAGRAM 11-3—Sometimes the shift of the defense to make the double team can be made as shown in this diagram. X2 teams up with X3 to two-time the inbounds pass receiver. When this happens X1 takes over the area in the middle of the court around the free throw circle. Otherwise, the defensive assignments and coverages are the same. If the offense is successful in moving the ball down floor the defense falls back into their normal defensive assignment in the 10 area or to their next line of defense. Any time the ball is passed down floor behind a defensive player, he must sprint toward the defensive basket until he is at least as deep as the ball. He will help where he can, and pick up the nearest offensive man that is free.

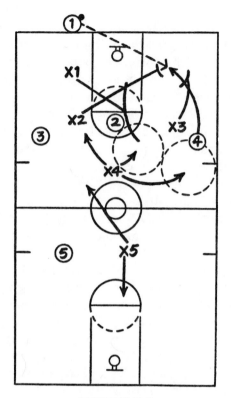

DIAGRAM 11-3

DIAGRAM 11-4, Phase 1—If the offense passes backward toward the end line, or makes cross court passes in this area, the defense is accomplishing its purpose, because the offense is not penetrating and they are consuming precious time on the 10-second count. If the offense passes back toward the end line and then later goes to the opposite side of the floor, the defense can still come up with a double team maneuver, as is shown in this and the following diagram. In this diagram X1 has forced the pass to the right side of the floor to 04. X3 now forces 04 away from the side line, and toward the middle, and into a trap situation with X1. X2 moves as shown, in toward the middle and around the free throw line area, and X4 and X5 are ready for moves into the areas indicated. 04 having no outlet pass down floor, passes the ball back toward the end line to 01 who, after passing inbounds to 04, has stepped inbounds. X1 and X3 will now do a release movement from

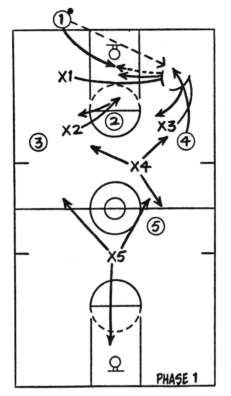

DIAGRAM 11-4—PHASE 1

04, adjusting slightly to be ready for the next pass, and to apply another trap if possible. X1 will not actually move at 01, but will fake at him to get possible movement. Time is on the side of the defense, so 01 will have to make a move by either a pass or a driving dribble. In either case, all players, including X2, have done a release move to be ready to counter whatever 01 does. The next diagram shows the double shift possibilities.

DIAGRAM 11-5, Phase 2—This diagram is a continuation of Diagram 11-4, Phase 1. 01 now has the ball, having received it after passing inbounds to 04, and then stepping inbounds to receive a return pass from him. X1, after releasing on 04 in the trap to the right side, now fakes aggressively at 01, and 01 passes to 03 on the left side of the floor. X2 now moves over to cut off 03 and to turn him inside, and with

X1, they double team 03 in a trap play. X3 shifts over to zone the middle of the court area around the free throw circle. X4 is responsible for the area to his left and behind X3 and 03. X5 has his usual responsibility at the division line, and for the deep court defensive area. In all these pressing defenses, if the offense gets by the defense in vertical penetration, the defense falls back as rapidly as possible into the next line of defense.

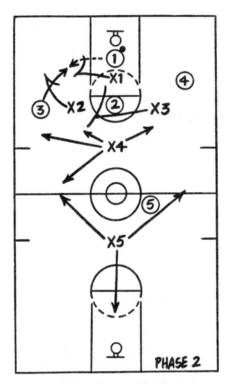

DIAGRAM 11-5—PHASE 2

DIAGRAM 11-6—The defense can slightly differ in positions at times, according to the offensive attack. X4 and X5 can vary their positions to work in almost parallel positions. The players must be taught to realize that if there is no opponent in their area or zone, they must shift more to the areas being attacked to help out. They will play pressure man-to-man when the opponent in their area has the ball, and float off in zone principles at other times—the distance of the float being determined by how far the man is from the ball. In this diagram, X2's responsibility is in the middle court area around the free throw circle. However, if there are no opponents in that area, he must shadow 02 more and be aware of movements 05 might make into the area to receive a possible pass from 03. A pass from 03 to 05 as shown in this diagram could be intercepted by X2 or X5. However, if X5 should move into this area of coverage, X4 must retreat to the deep defensive coverage that X5 has given up on this commitment. If X4 and X5 play as shown here, they must be prepared to exchange positions on this type of move.

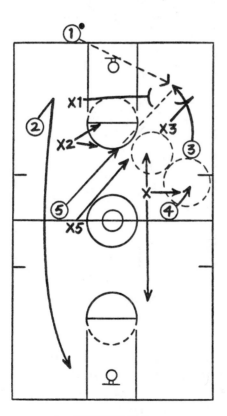

DIAGRAM 11-6

DIAGRAM 11-7—To show all possible passing situations and shifts would be endless. With the inbounds pass being made to 02 as shown in this diagram, the defense shifts as indicated. X4 and X5 might vary positions as shown by the shaded offensive and defensive player numbers, in case the offense should line up with 05 on the deep right side.

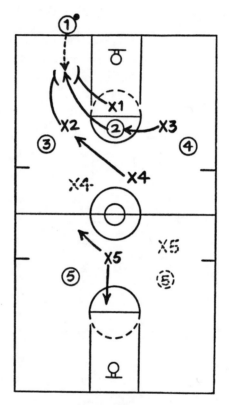

DIAGRAM 11-7

DIAGRAM 11-8—If the pass inbounds is made to 03 as shown in this diagram, the defensive shift is as shown. The possibilities of the coverage by X4 and X3 are given. X1 and X2 will double team 03. If 05, who began playing deep, should come up for a pass as shown, X5 may make a commitment with him for a while, but there comes a time when he must release him to X4, and if a player such as 04 is heading deep down court, X5 will have to come back fast for deep coverage.

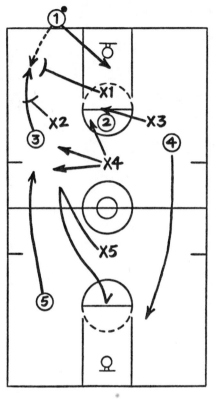

DIAGRAM 11-8

DIAGRAM 11-9—If the offensive player receiving the inbounds pass escapes the two-timing efforts of X2 and X1 as 03 has in this diagram, by dribbling down the outside, then X4 and X2 can team up on him down along the side line. X1 and X3 then shift as shown with X2 covering the middle court area from the free throw line and deeper, while X3 fills in the middle court area somewhat deeper, and to the left. X5 still looks to read the intent of the ball handler and plays for possible interceptions near the court division line and protects the deeper court areas.

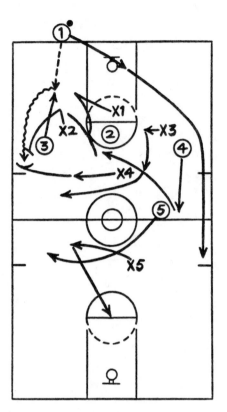

DIAGRAM 11-9

DIAGRAM 11-10—There are times when the defensive players will need to compensate their positions to make adjustments to the way the offense lines up. One of the most dangerous passes that can be made against this defense is a pass to the area of the court division line directly from out of bounds. In this diagram note that 03 and 04 are positioned near the court division line and 05 is deep in his front court area. X5 will have to read 01's intent carefully, and probably cannot be free to make a commitment into the middle court area with 05 playing so deep. If 01 should pass directly to 03 at the division line, the offense has an immediate outnumbering of the defense—a situation that could crack the defense immediately. To prevent this, X4 must compensate his position so as to be able to prevent this pass. Compensations by X2 and X3 should also be made as shown. X4 has a very challenging

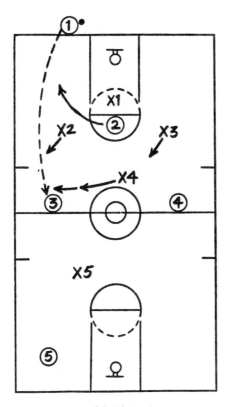

DIAGRAM 11-10

position to play here. He must have quick lateral movements, be able to read the intent of the ball handler, and be able also to make quick adjustments to prevent passes into this area. This is especially true when the offense lines up in this manner. Actually the pass is one to be invited, but the defense must be alert to intercept it.

When using this press, the players must be drilled to be aware of the change from offense to defense, and to effect this change quickly. This quick changing attitude will often catch the opponents unaware and help to capitalize on their errors. The whole idea of the defense is to get the opponents to make an error that will benefit the defensive team. The defense should encourage the opponents to dribble, and then drive the dribbler into a two-timing situation. When the ball moves by a defensive player toward the deep defensive area, he must be drilled in moving back toward the opponent's basket at sprint speed while sizing the situation up. On the way back he may chase a player from behind, knock a ball down toward a teammate, or pick up a possible situation that could bring about an offensive turnover. The pressure must be constant and tortuous, and always on the man with the ball. The 41 defense is a full blast, all-out pressure defense.

SECTION THREE

Alternate Defenses

12

THE NUMBER 10T, 14, AND 15 DEFENSES:
Combination Defenses

Section one of this book presented a defensive system that included 10 defenses with their many applications and variations. This chapter and the next one (chapters 12 and 13) will present some alternate defenses that could be used in addition to, or instead of some of the 10 defenses previously given. There are reasons for this additional presentation. There will be years when differing personnel will lend themselves better to another type of defense, or defenses. There will also be years when the team personnel will be able to handle more than the 10 defensive situations given, and the team can strengthen its game by using additional defenses.

The need to vary the zone presses in the 40 defensive full-court press area is also very acute at times, and the team will need to make adjustments in, or have additions to, the 41 defense. These defensive situations will be presented as the number 42, 43, and 44 defenses in chapter 13. Other special situations do occur and need special handling in defensive situations. Some of these will be presented as defenses 10T, 14, and 15 in this chapter.

THE 10T DEFENSE

The 10T defense is a team defense. It combines the man-to-man and the zone defenses in an attempt to make use of the strengths of both, while eliminating the weaknesses that each may have. It is also a position defense in that it attempts to keep certain defensive players next to the defensive board for rebounding purposes, while utilizing the aggressiveness of other players farther away from the basket. Being a position defense, it can also utilize fast break opportunities to the fullest while incorporating the strong points of the man-to-man defense. There will be years in the basketball program when the personnel on the team is such that it would be advantageous to play a 10T defense rather than a regular 10 defense described in chapter 2.

In the 10T defense, the focus of attention of the defensive players is to be divided between the man and the ball, but if one is to be favored more than the other, the defense should favor attention upon the ball. This is the fundamental difference between the regular 10 defense and the 10T defense. However, in every situation, every defensive player will be responsible for an opponent just as in the 10 defense.

Some very basic fundamental principles can be outlined for the 10T defense. They are as follows:

1. The emphasis of the defense is more upon the ball, yet each defensive player will have an assigned man at all times.
2. The defense will shift and help in switching situations so as to keep their original floor assignments and the same relative positions with respect to each other as much as possible. When not possible, the defensive player should move as needed to meet the situation. When pulled away from their normal position, the players should switch back as soon as possible.
3. The defense will originally line up to match the offensive alignment.
4. The defense will adjust their positions according to the movements of their opponents, but their focus of attention will always be on the ball.

The following diagrams will give the main ideas of how the defense works in its function as a team defense.

DIAGRAM 12-1, Phase 1—With the ball in possession of 01 at the position shown in this diagram, X1 plays the ball handler 01 tight. X2 and X3 play 02 and 03 a loose man-to-man, floating in toward the basket. They must be ready to move out on their opponent should he receive the ball. However, X4 and X5 play a zone position under the basket, being aware of the positions of 04 and 05 only. When the ball is passed from 01 to 02, the players shift as shown. X2 plays 02 tight man-to-man. X1 drops off 01 in a loose man-to-man. X5 shifts out toward 05 to a loose man-to-man position. Players X3 and X4 play a zone position, but must be aware of the position of 03 and 04, and never let them move into the scoring area ahead of them to meet the ball.

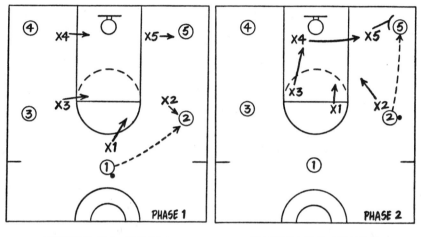

DIAGRAM 12-1—PHASE 1   DIAGRAM 12-2—PHASE 2

DIAGRAM 12-2, Phase 2—With the ball in possession of 02, the defense plays just as described in Diagram 12-1, Phase 1, on the pass from 01 to 02. When the ball is passed from 02 to 05, as shown in this diagram, X5 plays a tight man-to-man on 05, X2 drops off 02 in a loose man-to-man, and X1 drops farther into the zone area, but must be aware of 01 and his moves. X4 and X3 zone (float) the areas shown, but must still be aware of players 03 and 04, and be ready to stop or take any cutters moving into the area from the weak side toward the ball.

DIAGRAM 12-3, Phase 3—With the ball in possession of 05, the players have shifted to the positions shown in this diagram. If the ball is passed back to 02 from 05, the players shift back as indicated. Should the ball and play go to the left side of the floor, the shifts would be reversed to the opposite side.

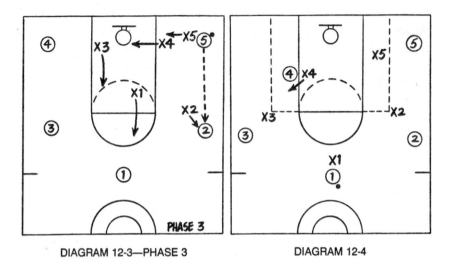

DIAGRAM 12-3—PHASE 3   DIAGRAM 12-4

DIAGRAM 12-4—If the offense should move a player into Area A—the vital scoring area—the defense must adjust accordingly. As shown in this diagram, 04 has moved into the pivot-post area. He now becomes the number one defensive problem. The defense must guard him tight man-to-man in this area, and play in front and on the side toward the ball at all times. The number two defensive problem now is the man with the ball. The emphasis is still on the ball, but with 04 in Area A, and the ball outside the area, emphasis is to prevent a pass into the area. The number three problem is the wing player, or the player breaking from the weak side toward the ball. X1 covers 01 tight man-to-man. X5 must drop off and zone behind X4 to give him as much help as possible. Players X2 and X3 play as deep as possible in a loose man-to-man, but must use judgment as to how far they can drop off, and still be in position to move quickly out to their opponent should he receive a pass from 01. X3 can assist X4 also in guarding 04. X1 plays to block any passes to 04 also.

DIAGRAM 12-5—If the ball should be passed from 01 to 03, and 05 should cut from the weak side to the strong side toward the ball as shown here, X5 must take him, but as he does so he should call to X2 to "watch behind." X2 now zones and is responsible for the right side of

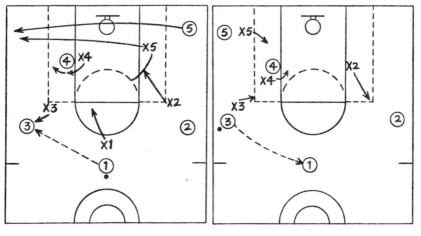

DIAGRAM 12-5

DIAGRAM 12-6

the court behind 04. He will rebound this area, and help on any floater "over-the-head" passes made to 04. He must also be aware of 02. X1, X3, and X4 shift as shown.

DIAGRAM 12-6—When the ball moves to 03 as shown here, the situation amounts to an offensive overload. Should 03 pass back to 01, X1 moves out tight on the ball. X3 drops off, alert to passes to 04, X5 loosens up on 05 to help X4, and X2 is still responsible to zone the right side. X2 stays inside 02, and must be ready to move out on him should he receive the ball. He must be ready to go in either direction to cover the situation.

DIAGRAM 12-7—Another way to give the idea of this defense is to take the ball at position 01, as shown in this diagram. From this position, picture an imaginary line from the ball to the basket. The defensive players group themselves about this line as closely as possible, concentrating upon the player with the ball, and attempt to read his actions and what he will do with it. At the same time they will be conscious of their defensive assignment or the player they are to guard. If the man they are guarding should receive the ball, they should be on the attack with him immediately. The farther their opponent is from the ball, the closer they can get to the imaginary line from the ball to the basket. In

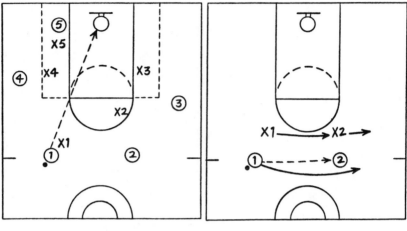

DIAGRAM 12-7   DIAGRAM 12-8

reverse of what has previously been said, it can also be said that the nearer the opponent is to the line connecting the ball with the basket, the closer the defensive player must play to him. This defense forces the offense out around the defense to the outside. It is a "20 principle" applied to the 10 defensive area. The positions of the defensive players will change with the movement of the ball and with the movement of their opponent. They must know the position of all the other players on the court, and as a consequence must develop a wide peripheral vision. They must know what is going on around them.

The defensive movements and positions will be governed by whether or not the offensive player is in a strong position where he can receive the ball with an opportunity to score. If he is in such a position, the defensive player must play close enough to the opponent to be able to attack him immediately should he get the ball, or to possibly intercept passes to him. If the offensive player is not in a strong position with respect to receiving the ball in the scoring area, then the defensive player can be less concerned about his movements and position. The defensive player can then hover closer about the line connecting the ball and the basket.

In the 10T defense, when it is possible to do so, the players shift opponents to keep their relative positions and alignment on the floor.

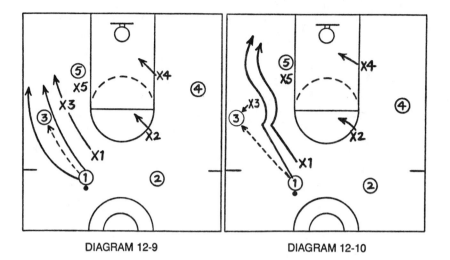

DIAGRAM 12-9   DIAGRAM 12-10

The idea is to place the players on the floor so that they will be the most effective in that particular position on the floor. When shifting can be done to keep these positions, they should do so, but when the situation is such that it cannot be done, then the defense plays accordingly.

DIAGRAM 12-8—This shows one of the many shifting possibilities. In general, the defense shifts whenever the players they are guarding cross in front of, or close to, them. This closeness is a judgment factor. This one is a simple shift and one that would be common where players cross or weave in a pattern out in front. Here 01 passes to 02 and then cuts behind him. X1 follows 01 across. When X1 and X2 come close enough to make contact, they shift, with X2 taking 01 and X1 shifting to guard 02.

DIAGRAM 12-9—If 01 should pass to 03 and take the paths shown here (either outside 03, or between 03 and X3) then X3 and X1 shift opponents as shown. X3, the defensive player nearest the basket calls the shift or help situation. This would be a very common shift situation. X1 and X3 work closely on the maneuver and talk constantly.

DIAGRAM 12-10—If 01 should pass to 03 and cut behind him as shown here, then X1 sticks in a tight man-to-man on 01. This is playing the

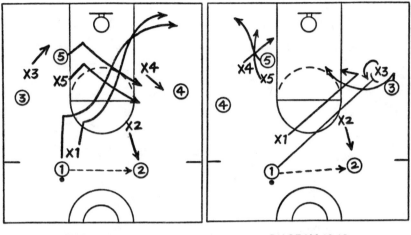

DIAGRAM 12-11   DIAGRAM 12-12

situation, and necessitates that X1 continue to guard 01. The other defensive players shift accordingly.

DIAGRAM 12-11—This is another situation where X1 would play the situation and stick by his man tight. 01 passes to 02, and cuts down the middle area as shown. The other defensive players make the adjustments shown. For a time here, X1 will be on the back line of defense rather than out in front in his original position. As long as the ball is in the position held by 02, X1 probably cannot shift back, but when the ball moves to the other side of the floor he will watch his chance to get back into position.

DIAGRAM 12-12—In the screen play shown in this diagram, X1 and X3 would shift as indicated. 01, after passing the ball to 02, takes a diagonal route behind X2. X1 drops back with 01. When 01 approaches 03, 03 cuts to the center as shown. X1 will shift to 03, and X3 will fight hard toward the center and back toward the basket so as to get between 01 and the basket.

DIAGRAM 12-13—Three things important to this defense are illustrated in this diagram. First, the defensive player should always guard the opponent in front of him, and have no worry about what is behind him.

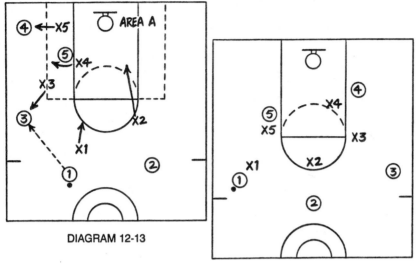

DIAGRAM 12-13

DIAGRAM 12-14

Here X5 can see a player in the corner and one under the basket. He must move out to guard 04, knowing that X4 will take 05. Second, any time an offensive player is in the dotted line area marked A, always play in front of him in a direct line between the opponent and the ball. The defense must have no worry about the pass over the defensive player's head for a score. The teammates sagging in can help enough on this to prevent this from being a danger. When the opponent moves out of Area A, the defense then must play behind him in the usual manner. Third, when the ball is passed behind a defensive player, he should drop off toward the basket until he is on a line level with the ball. Here, when 01 passes to 03, X1 immediately drops back on a line level with the ball. This move masses the defense about the imaginary line as previously mentioned, and prevents X1's opponent from driving around him. X1 is also in a better rebound position and a more sound defensive position. X2, who had previously dropped off his man, can sag in deeper toward the basket as the ball is passed from 01 to 03.

DIAGRAM 12-14—The defense will always line up to meet the offensive alignment and formation. This diagram shows how they would meet the double post offense.

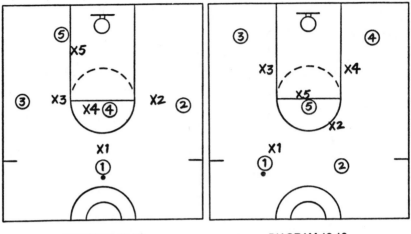

DIAGRAM 12-15   DIAGRAM 12-16

DIAGRAM 12-15—To meet the 1-3-1 offensive alignment the defense lines up as shown in this diagram. Each offensive opponent is accounted for.

DIAGRAM 12-16—This diagram shows the defense against the 2-1-2 offensive formation. The defense converges about the imaginary line from the ball to the basket, yet each defensive opponent is accounted for.

Commenting further on the 10T defense, the defense should always be formed from the basket—which is another way of saying that if an offensive player is to be left open, he should always be the one farthest from the basket. When the opponents use a fast break attack, the first two, three, or four players back on defense should form the defense nearest the basket, regardless of their normal assignments. When the other players get back, the defense will shift into their regular defensive positions at the first safe opportunity.

The 10T defense must be a highly coordinated team effort.

THE 14 DEFENSE

The 14 defense is a special defense used for a special situation, or to combat an opponent with special talent. Almost every season, at least

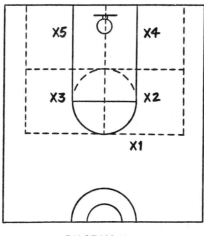

DIAGRAM 12-17

two to three times, the team will be faced with an opposing team who has one outstanding opponent whose scoring talents cannot be restrained or harnessed by one defensive player. Such superstars have to be handled by special defenses. The answer is a special defense such as the box zone plus one, which in this defensive system is called the 14 defense. When this situation is confronted, four men play a box zone near the basket inside what has been referred to previously as the 10 defensive area, while the fifth player plays a tight man-to-man against the superstar or high scorer. When the high-scoring opponent approaches the scoring zone, the one defensive player sticks him tight, harassing him at every move, knowing that should the opponent out-maneuver or beat him, he will have the support of the four-man box zone behind him to help him out and act as a stopgap. This will enable the one defensive player playing the tight man-to-man to go all out in his play to prevent the superstar opponent from scoring. Because of this back-up support to be given to him, he should first work hard to prevent the superstar from receiving the ball; and second, when he does secure the ball, he should play aggressively against him to prevent him from scoring.

DIAGRAM 12-17—This diagram shows how the box-one zone would line up. The dotted lines show the approximate zone coverage areas for X2, X3, X4 and X5. Accordingly, when in a zone defense, the players

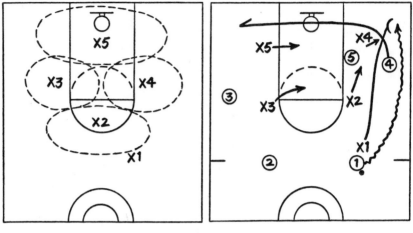

DIAGRAM 12-18   DIAGRAM 12-19

will in some situations shift to other zones when there are no opponents in their area, and of course toward the zone areas being attacked. X1 will guard the one high-scoring opponent tight and will take him as he comes into his scoring range, guarding him man-to-man wherever he goes.

DIAGRAM 12-18—Sometimes the 14 defense might want to line up as shown in this diagram in what might be referred to as a diamond-one. It is basically the same as the box-one, but aims to keep X5 closer to the basket to use his rebounding talents, and will expect a wider range of shifting by X3 and X4 to help out in the corner and side areas as needed. X2 should shift as needed, and again X1 will take the superstar tight man-to-man wherever he goes in the scoring area. The diamond-one arrangement in the 14 will be used less frequently than the box-one, but should be used where the special talents of one player such as X5 might be exploited near the basket area.

DIAGRAM 12-19—As shown in this diagram, the high-scoring opponent may be a guard. Here 01 is the opponent that must be stopped. X1 stays with him wherever he goes. If he should dribble down the outside to the baseline, the defense would shift as shown, as X1 stays tight on

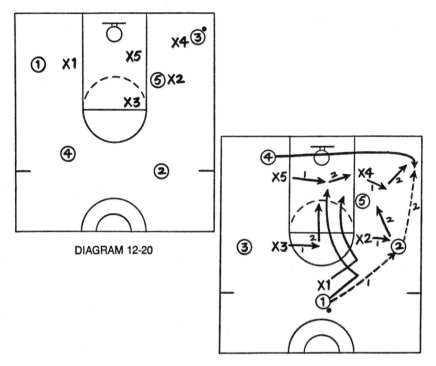

DIAGRAM 12-20

DIAGRAM 12-21

01. The shifts of the four other defensive players will be determined by the position of the ball, the opponents in their area, and the nearness of their area to the point of attack.

DIAGRAM 12-20—If the ball should be moved to 03 in the position shown in this diagram, and 01 (the superstar) should move to the weak side away from the ball, X1 will play as shown, always making sure he is ready to prevent 01 from receiving the ball, and being sure he is ready to guard him tight should he receive the ball.

DIAGRAM 12-21—In this diagram 01 is the superstar to be stopped. X1 guards him. When 01 passes to 02, the defense shifts as indicated. With the second pass from 02 to 04 the players shift as shown. X1 plays 01 tight as he breaks through the middle.

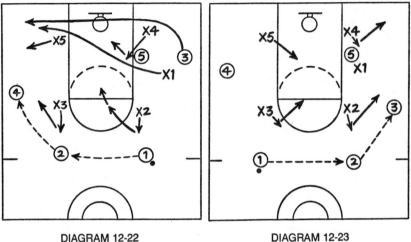

DIAGRAM 12-22   DIAGRAM 12-23

DIAGRAM 12-22—The superstar player to stop could be a forward such as 03, shown in this diagram. X1 guards him tight and close. When the ball moves from 01 to 02 to 04, the defense shifts as shown in the box. As 03 moves toward the ball X1 should play him in such a manner as to keep him from getting the ball in Area A, and to be in a tight guarding position at all times.

DIAGRAM 12-23—The superstar to be stopped could be a pivot-post player. If this were the case, the box-one could still be used, and X1 would play directly between 05 (the superstar) and the ball, fronting him at all times when he is in Area A. Playing 05 in this manner assures having a defensive player in front of and behind him at all times when he is in this area. If 05 should move out of the area, X1 should drop into the normal tight guarding position to prevent him from receiving the ball if at all possible. If 05 should receive the ball, X1 will harass him to the utmost.

DIAGRAM 12-24—This diagram shows how, if the diamond-one is used in the 14 defense, X3 and X4 are expected to do a wider coverage on the sides and in the corners. X1 still plays the superstar tight—in this

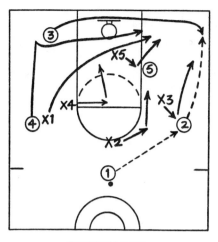

DIAGRAM 12-24

case 04. Actually, the center area in the pivot-post area will be left as the weakest coverage area, but should 04 break into this area, with X1 guarding him tight, X4 and X5 should be able to give plenty of help.

THE 15 DEFENSE

The 15 defense is another special situation defense and could be called a combination defense. In the 15 defense three men zone the area near the basket, and two defensive men play man-to-man. This defense would be used most often against a team that had two outstanding guards that are to be classed as superstars. The problem of the defense would be the guards. It could be used in other situations where the superstars might be one guard and one forward, or perhaps in rare situations where the combination might be a guard and the center or a forward and the center. The diagrams will give the shift possibilities and how they should be played.

DIAGRAM 12-25—In this diagram the dotted lines show the zone areas to be guarded by X3, X4 and X5 in the 15 defense. X1 and X2 take the two guards who are outstanding scorers man-to-man wherever they go.

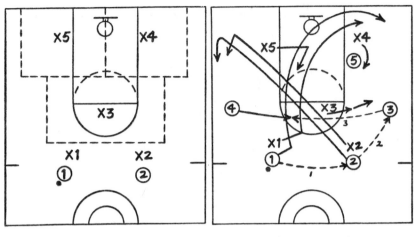

DIAGRAM 12-25   DIAGRAM 12-26

They should stick them tight and pressure them excessively because if they are outmaneuvered, they will have the three zone defense players behind them to back them up.

DIAGRAM 12-26—Admittedly there are very definite weaknesses to a defense such as the 15 defense combination of 3 zone and 2 man-to-man players. However, the objective of the defense is to stop the two high scorers, which in this case are the guards, 01 and 02. X1 and X2 guard them tight and aggressive wherever they go. The defense will gamble on the other players being ineffective enough on shots from a range of 15 to 20 feet from the basket that it will produce a plus for them. In this diagram, a simple move as shown could easily clear 04 for a shot near the free throw circle area. His ineffectiveness from this range will be the gamble the defense must take. Note that when 01 and 02 drive through, X1 and X2 have gone with them.

DIAGRAM 12-27—The two outstanding superstars could be a guard and a forward to be played man-to-man. As shown in this diagram, 02 and 03 are the high scorers to be stopped and X1 and X2 play them tight man-to-man when they come within the scoring range. In a situation as illustrated here, with 03 being on the right side of the floor, X3 will play strong to the left side of his zone area to be nearer threats from 01

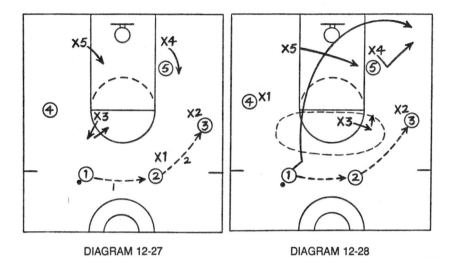

DIAGRAM 12-27   DIAGRAM 12-28

or 04. By cooperating and sliding properly, X5, X4 and X3 can keep the areas near the basket well guarded, and give help to X1 and X2 as needed. There are many patterns and combinations possible—too numerous to be diagrammed, but the main ideas are expressed here.

DIAGRAM 12-28—If the two outstanding scorers to be stopped are both forwards, it will require a very active response from the defensive player in X3's position. He will have to be very active in combatting activity in the dotted area, and if both guards should cut through toward the basket, X3 will have to go with the second cutter to give aid to X4 and X5, who could be outmaneuvered on an overload near the basket. X3 can move back to his position as soon as one guard returns to the outside. X1 and X2 play the forwards 04 and 03 tight man-to-man wherever they go.

DIAGRAM 12-29—The high-scoring duo could be a pivot-post player and a forward, or a pivot-post player and a guard. The 15 defense in a 3 zone, 2 man-to-man combination can still be applied in this situation. X1 should defense 05 and front him on the side of the ball any time he plays inside defensive Area A. This almost assures a defensive player being in front of, and behind 05 at all times. X2 then sticks the forward 03 tight in a man-to-man. With this situation and X1 playing in front of 05

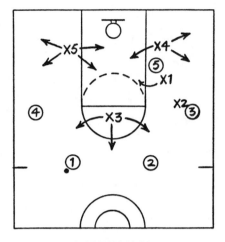

DIAGRAM 12-29

in defensive Area A, X3 will have more coverage to the top of the circle and to his right or left to help out as needed in these areas, since with X1 in the area, four defensive men would be in the area very close unless X3 covered a wider range. If the combination of scorers were the pivot-post player and a guard, such as 02, then X2 would guard 02 man-to-man and X3 would adjust his lateral movements accordingly.

STUNTING DEFENSES AND THE 15 DEFENSE

In some rare situations the 15 defense, which is a combination defense of 3 zone 2 man-to-man combination, could be broadened in its stunting range to include such stunts as a 2 man zone with 3 men playing man-to-man, and even a one man zone near the basket with the other four men playing a man-to-man defense. Each of these is a very special situation and will need to be worked out to fit the personnel of the opponents, and the offense that they work. It is well to be aware of such stunting possibilities and to know how they can be put into effect. Such stunting activities can be very upsetting to the offensive team at times and are well worth the trial effort needed to get the team to use them. With a little work and experimentation, the defensive team can make the various adjustments needed in the many combinations and stunt defenses as the occasion arises.

13

THE NUMBER 42, 43, AND 44 DEFENSES:
Variations of the Zone Press

In chapter 11, the number 41 defense was presented as a basic full-court zone press defense. This chapter will present three other *zone press defenses* that can be used in the place of the 41 defense, or as additional defenses. The basic principles and concepts of the zone presses are the same. The only difference is in the player alignment on the court at the beginning of the defenses. Like the 41 defense, the 42, 43, and 44 defenses are full-court zone pressing defenses. As has been explained before, any defense numbered in the 40's will be a full-court press.

Another important point to remember is that regardless of the original lineup or alignment of the defensive players, after the first pass and when the trap is applied, the defense will have two players on the ball, two players floating and converging on passing lanes, and one player back for defense. This means that after the first move, almost all zone press defenses will in effect be in a 2-2-1 alignment. They may start out differently, but they end up the same.

The additional options to the zone press defense are presented because there will be moments in the defensive battle when an application of the players in a different arrangement can give the combination necessary to solve the offensive thrust. Sometimes, too, the personnel available in a defensive unit will work more efficiently in a certain combination or alignment. For this reason, the coach should certainly experiment to possibly find the best arrangement for his players, and to find out if his players can possibly handle more than one zone press alignment. The ability to confront the offense with different alignments and arrangements in the press application can add to their confusion, and be just the added impetus that is needed to bring about an offensive dilemma that will cause a rout. When the right defensive combination is finally discovered, the opponents can panic in confusion, and give up an avalanche of points in a short time that can be the margin of victory.

THE NUMBER 42 DEFENSE

The number 42 zone press defense is a 2-1-2 full-court zone press. The 2-1-2 alignment will give a stronger position for the defense in the middle court area, and down the middle. It could be just what is needed to spring the necessary two-timing situations, and bring the confusion to the offense that will cause them to throw the long pass, commit a violation, or give up a held ball. It also will give the very excellent coverage deep down court, while still giving all the pressure possibilities of a full-court press. If the opponents have an exceptionally tall or strong player in the middle, the defense may need to go to this alignment to combat the first or second pass to him. With strength in the middle, this defense would also be one to use when, for reasons revealed by scouting reports, or other, it is desirable to definitely force the opponent to the areas away from the middle of the court and toward the side lines.

DIAGRAM 13-1—The 42 zone press alignment is shown in this diagram. It should present strength in the middle, and force the offense to the side lines. The defense would take this formation when the offensive team has been successful in making their first passes inbounds to the area occupied by X3, or when the offense has an especially tall or strong and effective player receiving passes in this area. The dotted line divisions on the court show the beginning coverage areas for each player. Note the broad lateral coverage for X3. The arrows give the movement possibilities for each player. Naturally, in any zone press defense, there will be overlapping of zone coverage areas for all of the players.

DIAGRAM 13-2—If the pass inbounds is to the area shown in this diagram, X1 should force 02 to the outside and team up with X3 to

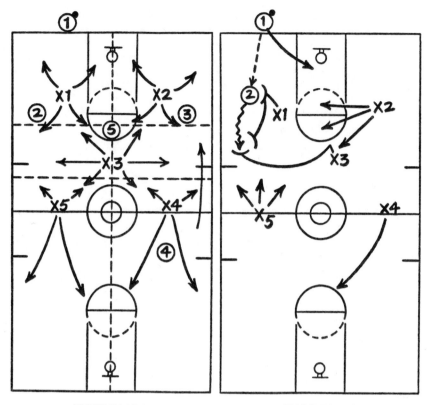

DIAGRAM 13-1   DIAGRAM 13-2

two-time 02. X2 and X5 float or zone the passing areas back of, and to the right of, X3 to intercept passes. Their shift possibilities are shown. X4 covers the deep defensive area.

DIAGRAM 13-3—If the pass inbounds should be maneuvered in such a manner as to cause the trap play to be away from the side line and to the middle, as shown in this diagram, the defense should shift as shown. X1 and X2 would apply the trap, with X5 and X3 covering the passing lanes while X4 should play back for defense and protect against the cheap basket. If the offense should come from the opposite side of the court, then X5 and X4 would exchange positions in this maneuver.

DIAGRAM 13-4—If the offense should line up as shown in this diagram,

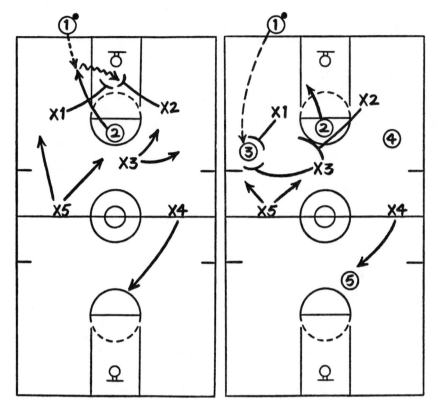

DIAGRAM 13-3   DIAGRAM 13-4

with 01 taking the ball out on the left side of the basket, and 05 being deep down court, X4 should move back at once for the back position. If 01 should be on the right side of the basket, then X5 would make this move. If 01 should pass inbounds to 03 at the position shown, X1 and X3 would work for the trap on him, with X5 and X2 covering the passing lanes for interceptions. As soon as the trap is applied, the defense has shifted in reality to a 2-2-1 zone press. These diagrams show the basic shifts of the 42 defense.

THE NUMBER 43 DEFENSE

The number 43 defense is a 3-2 full-court zone press. It would be used in a situation where the defense would want to force the offense away from the side line and into a trap toward the middle. Such situations do

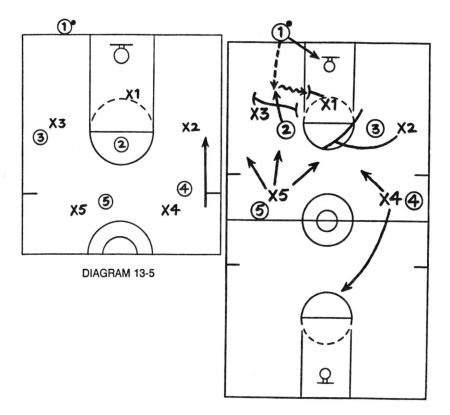

DIAGRAM 13-5

DIAGRAM 13-6

occur, and would give the defense the weapon it needs to further confuse and confound the offense. It would also be a consideration when the offense presents little or no strength in the middle, or at least poses no threat there with an outlet pass. Another possibility for its use and application would be when there is no danger of a long deep pass down court.

DIAGRAM 13-5—This diagram shows the basic 43 alignment of the players. X1, X2, and X3 should vary their depth of position according to the position of the opponents. X4 and X5 will also vary in depth. If the ball is taken to the left side of the basket for the throw-in, X4 will cover the deep defensive area. If the ball is taken to the right side of the basket, X5 will cover the deep defensive area. The idea in this defense is to have X3 and X2 prevent moves toward the side line and to force

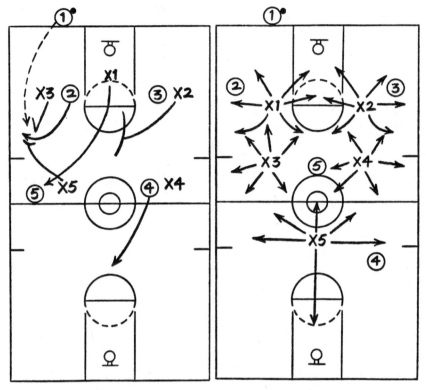

DIAGRAM 13-7   DIAGRAM 13-8

the ball handler toward the middle where traps can be applied with the help of X1. Another situation calling for this defense would be when the defensive team has a player in the X1 position who is especially adept in the trap situation in making clean steals, and in other harassing movements that pressure the dribbler and ball handler.

DIAGRAM 13-6—If the ball is passed in to 02 as shown in this diagram, X3 forces 02 away from the side line, and toward X1 where X3 and X1 double team him in a trap. X2 and X5 move to cover the passing lanes and float as shown. X4 plays deep if needed. The defense has now actually shifted to a 2-2-1 zone alignment.

DIAGRAM 13-7—If 01 should pass deep down the side line, and over the head of the first line of the defense as shown in this diagram, then X3 and X5 team up to double team 02. X1 and X2 must react quickly, and reading the ball handler, be on their way fast and early to cover the proper passing lanes. X1 should guard the lanes behind X5, and X2 should cover the middle passing areas. X4 must quickly cover the deep defensive area.

THE NUMBER 44 DEFENSE

The number 44 defense is a 2-2-1 full-court zone press. After the first pass and the application of the trap situation, most of the other zone presses become 2-2-1 alignments anyway. With this alignment of players, it begins as it usually ends. It presents a strong front court alignment for the defensive team, while giving adequate deep court defensive coverage. If weak anywhere, it might present some weakness in the middle of the defense between the top of the free throw circle and the center circle. This defense should probably be the first to be considered as one to be used with the 41 defense, or in some cases, instead of it, if only one zone press is to be in the defensive repertory.

DIAGRAM 13-8—This diagram presents the basic alignment of the 44 defense—a full-court zone press defense. The trap can be applied either along the side line or away from the side line. Regardless of where the trap is applied, two players will be acting on the trap situation; two players will be behind this action floating, zoning and playing for interceptions in the passing lanes; and one player will be back deep for defense against the long pass and the cheap basket.

DIAGRAM 13-9—This diagram shows a trap away from the side line. With the ball taken out to the left of the basket as indicated, the defense will invite the offense to pass into the area somewhere in front of X1. X1 should then advance on the ball handler, and force him into a trap situation with X2. X3 will be responsible for the passing lanes behind the trap from the center line to the foul line on his side of the floor. X4 is responsible for covering the middle of the floor to his left and on his side from the center to the foul line. X2 should discourage passes inbounds to his side of the floor, and then be ready to move in with a double-team action on 02 with X1. X5 directs defense from near the center circle area, and is responsible for any player down court, and is expected to intercept any long passes made to the deep defensive area.

DIAGRAM 13-10—If 02 should receive the ball and drive down the side

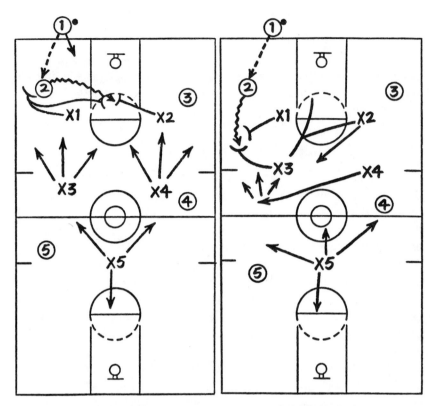

DIAGRAM 13-9   DIAGRAM 13-10

line past X1, then X3 must be prepared to stop this driver, and with X1 apply a two-timing situation on 02 as shown in this diagram. X2 and X4 shift as shown. X4 covers the passing lanes behind the trap, on the left side of the floor. X2 must be responsible for the area from the free throw line to the center circle on the right side of the court. X5 directs the defensive play from the center circle as usual, and takes care of the deep defensive coverage area.

DIAGRAM 13-11—The 44 defense gives plenty of upcourt defensive strength but occasionally the offense may be able to make the first pass inbounds into the middle. If this should happen as shown in this diagram, X2 and X4 should two-time the ball handler (he is nearest them). X3 should guard the passing lanes behind them and to his right. X1 should fall back and float in the passing lanes from the top of the circle to the center line through the center and left side of the court. X5 should play from the center of the court and back as needed.

When the offense penetrates the defense and brings the ball down to their own front court, the defense falls back and assembles in whatever defense they are running at the time.

The defense must always be alert to make changes in position and alignment according to the position taken on the court by the offense. As soon as the ball is passed inbounds, the defense can then make the necessary shifts and changes to double-team the ball handler, float and cover the passing lanes, and have a defensive player back to protect against the cheap basket.

All full-court pressing defenses take much work, drill, discipline, and patience on the part of the players and the coach.

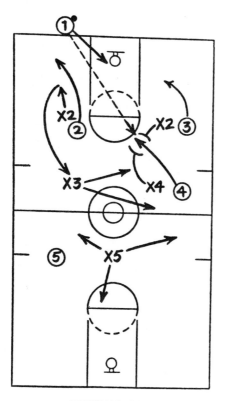

DIAGRAM 13-11

14

Cycling or Rotating the Defenses

A cycle is any round of operations or events, or a series that returns upon itself. Cycling the defenses is rotating them as a series or a round. To put it another way, it is alternating or rotating the defenses using a series or a cycle of different defenses. To do this means that the offense will constantly face a different defense every time they gain possession of the ball.

The basic philosophical thinking behind the defensive system presented in this book is to present the fundamental defensive concepts necessary to play multiple defenses. These fundamental concepts were followed with 10 applications of those concepts. Optional possibilities or additions were also explained. Some coaches and basketball buffs will be inclined to think it is impossible for a high school or a college team to master and apply 10 different defenses. A casual glance or thought on the subject might cause one to think like this, but further scrutiny reveals the fallacy of such thinking. It must be remembered that the basic concepts for all team defenses, while stressing the defensive play of the individual, and while basically man-to-man, constantly stress the necessity of including both zone and man-to-man principles in the team defenses. In reality there is very little difference in the fundamental ideas presented in any of the defenses, regardless of whether it is man-to-man, a zone, a combination, or a press. The difficulty then becomes that of mastering the fundamental concepts. Once this is done, the team can easily make at least 10 applications of the concepts, and in a great many cases teams will be able to play all the defenses presented in this book and readily shift from one defense to another by clue or signal. The coach has to be reasonable, however, and it is doubtful if a freshman team in high school, or a junior high school team could play this number of defenses, but if properly taught and drilled, they will be able to·do many of the applications, and shift from one defense to another.

Analyzing this still further, the number 10 defense is basically a man-to-man defense incorporating zone principles in floating, sagging, and sluffing off from the weak side toward the middle. It further emphasizes pressure at the point of the ball, a *no no* through the middle, with very little switching. The 20, 30, and 40 defenses are fundamentally and basically the same, except for the point of contact where the defense begins to pressure the offense, and in that the offense is to be forced toward the side line rather than away from it as in the 10 defense. The "10-principle" and the "20-principle" have both been explained and can be used to add variety to each defense. The "20-principle" can be applied to the 10 defense, and the "10-principle" can be applied to the 20, 30, and 40 defenses. This can easily be done on a clue or a verbal signal.

The 10T defense differs from the regular 10 defense only in that it is more a *position* defense, incorporates more switching and shifting to maintain desirable player positions on the floor, and it applies the "20-principle" to the 10 defensive area.

Every team should have at least one zone defense that it can apply to the 10 defensive area, and every team should have full-court zone pressing defenses in its defensive repertory. The first and easiest zone defense to teach for the 10 defensive area would be the number 11 defense. The positions and shifts are simple and easy to learn. After the 11 defense, the 12 and the 13 defenses could be added as the defensive abilities of the team develop.

The first pressing defense to be taught should always be a man-to-man defense. This falls in easily with the 20, 30, and the 40 defenses. When the team has mastered these pressure defenses, it should be ready for the zone presses. The 41 and the 31Z should be the first presented. If the team has mastered the fundamental concepts, it should be able to easily handle the zone presses. After the 41 defense, probably the next full-court press should be the 44 defense. The other defenses such as the 14, 15, 31, 42, and 43 can be added as needed or as the team shows the ability to handle the added defensive repertory.

The last few years have seen tremendous developments in the offensive game of basketball. Even more revolutionary have been the trends in defense. Multiple defenses are here—the trend has been and will continue to be one of constantly changing defenses. The days when you can scout an opponent and prepare for one defense are past. All these techniques are now applied in defense—alternating defenses, rotating defenses, combination defenses, match-up defenses, concealed defenses, defenses by rule, zone defenses, man-to-man defenses, full-court pressure defenses, three-fourths-court pressure defenses, half-court pressure defenses, tactical defenses, special situation defenses, and defenses by clue. All these defenses come with variations, and in different varieties, with flexibilities for each. It makes it tough for the offense. The day when the team can have one offensive formation or attack for a man-to-man defense and another for a zone defense is also past. The team must now, almost of necessity, have an offensive attack that operates against all types of defenses.

The defense must never allow an offensive team to feel that they can operate with freedom and have a continuous style or patterned offense that can do what it wants to do. Constantly changing, alternating or cycling defenses can accomplish this. Each change in the defensive pattern should disturb the opponents and cause them to have to make a change or an adjustment. After a time the opponents can become so engrossed in adjustment and change that they accomplish little else. The defense should call the tricks—the tempo, and the tone of the game. Such a defensive team will win.

Another argument that can be given for the multiple defensive system and for applying it in cycles or by rotation, or constantly changing it, is that while it is possible to overcoach a team on offense, this is not true on defense. Overcoaching reflects itself in tensions that quickly affect and reflect themselves in ball handling, cutting and shooting. Not so on defense. The defense cannot be overcoached, but if such a word could be used it would reflect itself in a more alert, a more intent, and a more aggressive defensive team. This is good. This is why the coach can emphasize, and can coach defense constantly, and have no fear of overcoaching this phase of the game.

How can the team cycle or rotate the defenses? There are several ways it could be done. The team using such a system should have a defensive captain. The defensive captain should call the defensive switches or changes. He can make the calls verbally by audible signals or by other clues. There is no fault in simply just calling out the number of the defense to be used and having the number repeated by the other team members. This is a method that makes the understanding complete.

The team should enter the game with a defensive plan. The plan can be the result of scouting reports, or factors known about the opponents. A cycle of defensive changes can be predetermined so that the changes would be automatic under certain situations. By cycling or rotating defenses, the team can hope to hide the real defense being used at times—to confuse the opponent so that they do not know what defense they are operating against. If such concealment could be effective for only a short time, it could be the margin that gives the win.

DEFENSIVE CYCLES TO RUN

The team could run a man-to-man cycle, or rotate the man-to-man defenses by numbers. Such a cycle would be to rotate in numerical order the so-called man-to-man defenses in the system. In this case it would be a rotation of the 10, 20, 30, and 40 defenses, rotating them so that every time the opposition got the ball, they would be confronted by the application of the defense at a different point on the court. Usually the 40 series of numbered defenses is applied only after a score, or the awarding of the ball to the opponents deep in their own back-court or along the end-line. If the team has mastered the 10T defense, the 10T could be added to this cycle, so that these defenses could be applied in this order against the opponents—10, 10T, 20, 30, and 40.

Another cycle to run would be the *press cycle*. To do this the team would simply rotate by numerical order the pressing defenses that are in the team's defensive repertory. It could be a rotation of the defenses such as the 20, 30, 31, 31Z, 40, 41, and 44. This way the opponents would have to constantly adjust to differing pressure defenses as they bring the ball down the floor.

The team could also run an *area cycle*. This would be a rotation and constant changing of the defenses in the 10 defensive area. Such an area cycling of the defenses would run like this—10, 10T, 11, 12, 13, and possibly 15, or even 14, on occasion, being included in the rotation and changing of the defenses. In this particular area cycle, the opponents would simply be faced with a different defense in the 10 defensive area each time they brought the ball down the court. Another area cycle could be 30, 31, 31Z, rotated at the 30 area or application point. The 40 area presses could also be cycled by rotating 40, 41, 42, 43, and 44, or whatever full-court presses the team has in its repertoire of defenses.

A *zone cycle* could also be run. The zone defenses could be the "cup of tea" for some teams. The team will meet opponents who cannot handle a zone defense properly and in these cases the best weapon the team could have on defense would be the zone defenses. The zones could be cycled within an area, or a full cycle of all zone defenses could be run. Within an area, the zones 11, 12, 13, 14, and 15 could be rotated—all of them, or as many as the team wants to include in the rotation. It could also run 11, 12, 13, 31, 31Z, and 41, and include others if needed. A predetermined plan can always decide what to include in the defensive cycle.

An indiscriminate cycle could also be used. In this plan, the defensive captain with the aid of the coach would call the defensive rotation, making changes as the need dictated itself on the court according to the progress of the game. The situation in the game would dictate the defense, and the captain would call the change according to pre-arranged signals.

The team could also run one cycle for one quarter or a half, and then change cycles for the next period. A high school team could run one cycle during the first quarter, another the second quarter, and determine the cycles to be used during the second half at the half-time intermission.

Many teams, when on offense, still use different offensive attacks or completely different systems for a zone defense and a man-to-man defense. Such teams will often attack a man-to-man defense with a two-man front (two guards) and a zone defense with a one-man front. This gives the multiple defensive team an excellent clue as to how to rotate their defenses. When the offense comes down floor with a two-man front, the defensive team could switch to one of the zone defenses. When the offense presents a one-man front, the defense should switch back to the 10, or the 10T defense. Such tactics can keep the offensive team in a state of constant confusion. Keeping the opponents in such a dilemma for a period of two or three minutes at times can furnish the margin necessary for victory.

DEVELOPING THE ABILITY TO CYCLE

To develop the ability to cycle or rotate the defenses, the team must practice and be drilled in the techniques of shifting from one defense to another. With practice and drill, the team can make the changes without a hitch or a fault. Such play calls for complete unity of team play and thought, but here is where the basis of a real team unit can be formed. Such team unity and thinking will carry over to the offense, and add to and solidify the team concept in every phase of the game.

One way to drill and practice on the cycling of the defenses would be to practice the changing of the defenses during practice scrimmages, with team captains (defensive) giving the signals or verbal calls, thus giving the team the constant practice in such techniques. Changes should be made in the defenses according to pre-arranged cycles or according to the strategy appropriate at the time.

Special drills could also be worked out that would give the team

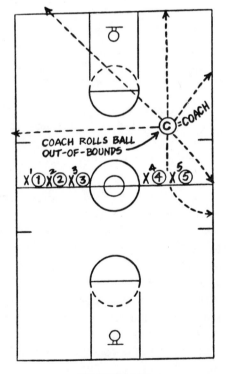

DIAGRAM 14-1

practice in cycling, rotating, and shifting from one defense to another. Such a drill devised for this purpose is shown in Diagram 14-1. It is a competitive drill, and gives continuous practice in cycling and constantly changing the defenses.

DIAGRAM 14-1—The players line up at the court division line, alternating players on the teams. The two teams for scrimmage purposes will have different colored shirts. The coach will take the ball and call the shirt color of the team that is to go on offense. He will then roll the ball out of bounds where they are to take the ball out and go on offense. The other team then has the defensive captain call the defense to be used, and will go on defense. The defensive captain calls the defenses according to the spot where the ball is out of bounds, or according to a pre-arranged cycle. To make the drill more interesting and competitive, a score could be kept with the following rules in effect:

— The coach varies the calls for the offense and defense so that the teams will have about equal chances on each.
— The team on offense is limited to 30 seconds possession, or to 3 shots, whichever occurs first. When a team scores or the time limit expires, the teams reassemble at the court division line again. The coach makes another call and another roll of the ball.
— A basket counts 2 points.
— If the team on defense steals the ball, they are limited to 20 seconds possession, or 2 shots, whichever occurs first.
— A steal by the defense counts 1 point.
— If the defense forces a violation or a bad pass, score 1 point.
— If either team fouls, score 1 point for opponents.
— If the offensive team takes a poor shot or a hurried shot, score 1 point for opponents.

With this drill, keep score for a time limit of from 7 to 10 minutes, or longer if the coach feels the need for it. The coach will vary the spots where the ball is taken out of bounds and give the team practice in cycling and rotating defenses while engaging in an enthusiastic competitive drill. The managers or assistants can keep score. This drill is also an excellent one for the offense in that it gives practice against the changing defenses while developing the offensive play from end line to end line.

15

Defensive Attitude

By now it should be clear that the authors consider defense in basketball to be an extension of the offensive phase of the game. There must be some way to get the ball back without giving up a score. The answer to this is *by excellent defensive play*, making it an extension of the offensive arm. This is especially true when the team goes into pressure defenses attempting to force the opponents into a turnover that will give the ball back. This brings up an old adage in reverse—"The best offense is a good defense." A good defense means more ball possession time for the offense, and this should mean more scoring.

Many words or phrases are used to describe a championship team. Usually it comes out with such words as discipline, character, pride, intestinal fortitude, determination, teammanship, and balanced effort. All these descriptive terms are those that would be used to describe a team that has the defensive attitude. It is, in fact, hard to imagine a team being a champion without having the *defensive attitude*. Real championship teams do have a balanced effort between offense and defense, and thus must have the *attitude* necessary to play good defense.

The coach will have to develop the defensive attitude. He will have plenty of help in the offensive phase of the game. Offense is the *attention getter* of the game. Everyone talks about this phase of the game. The coach will have help from the newspapers, radio, TV, the fans, and the parents in developing the scoring machine. Everyone talks about the score, and how many baskets Johnnie made. The usual first question asked of a player by an admirer or a friend is, "How many did you get tonight?"—meaning baskets, of course. When players practice alone or on their own, what do they practice? It is always offense or shooting. Players are never seen working on the defensive phases of the game alone. The public in general know so little about the game, that they can recognize only the scorer. This means that if the defensive attitude is to be developed, the coach must do it. He will be alone in this "hard-sell" program until he gets the movement going. Even after it catches on, he will have to press continuously on the program of developing the defense.

What are some of the things the coach will have to do to develop the defensive attitude? He will have to sell his defensive philosophy. To do this the coach must talk defense and emphasize defense constantly. The players will have enough talk among themselves and the townspeople about scoring, baskets, and the offense. He must give praise for superb defensive play at every opportunity, both in practice and in the games. No one else will give such praise because they do not know that much about the game. They can't recognize a fine piece of defensive work, so the coach owes it to the player making a fine defensive effort to give him every recognition possible.

The question is often raised as to how much time the coach should spend on defense in his practices. Except for the ball handling drills—whatever is done to develop the skills of passing, dribbling, and shooting—the coach should spend as much time practicing defense as he does offense. This could vary with each squad, and with the developmental phases of the team, but as a general rule, except for the time spent on drills developing ball handling skills, the coach ought to spend as much time working on defense as on offense. This means, of course, that more practice time will be spent developing the offensive phases of the game. It must also be remembered that while the team is working on defense, usually they are also working on some phase of offense. The coach, while working on offensive techniques and tactics more, should emphasize defense more.

To bring the team around to his defensive attitude and to ingrain his defensive philosophy into the public, the coach can do several things. One "gimmick" is through competitive defensive drills. Through such drills, the coach could select each week a "Defensive Player of the Week." This could be done by a one-on-one tournament, awarding the player that held opponents to the least number of baskets. Other means of selecting this player could also be devised. Of course the recipient of this award must be given some recognition that will cause it to be much sought after. It could be the player's name posted in a prominent place in school, newspaper recognition, a pair of socks, or some such recognition.

The coach should select a defensive captain for the squad. The selection of such a person should be carefully made, and based on this player's willingness to promote and generate a continuous flow of defensive ideas throughout the squad the entire season. This captain should be responsible for defenses during the games for cycling and changing the defenses as needed as the game progresses.

At the end of the year the coach should give an award for the following:

1. The best defensive player of the year.
2. The most improved defensive player of the year.

Appropriate newspaper publicity and coverage should be given such awards. By a continuous campaign of his own, and with the cooperation of reporters and other people, the coach will find that in time his efforts to inculcate the defensive attitude will be rewarded. When he hears the talk in the locker room centering around how a certain opponent is to be defensed in the upcoming game, he will know that he is getting results.

The coach should search continuously and overlook no chance for an opportunity to improve the defensive attitude of the team. He must develop in each individual a desire to play good defense. Individual pride will carry over to pride in good team defense.

A player who has offensive talent also has defensive talent. In fact, it takes more natural "God-given" talent to play offense than defense. A player who stars on offense, but performs poorly on defense usually neglects his defense, and wants to give time and thought to that phase of the game that will give him the most recognition. Such a player lacks pride and character. Defense takes more intestinal fortitude, more character, more determination, and exemplifies more maturity in the individual and the team. The coach should constantly promote that idea, and praise and give recognition accordingly. The coach, in instilling defensive pride in the players, can point out that anyone can shoot the ball, but a player must be real great to play defense so that it is noticed. All must have enough character to play both phases of the game.

It is also true that there are many talented athletes who do not have the "God-given" talent to be awesome scorers. These players, because of their athletic ability, can play superb defense. Any good athlete can play defense if he will concentrate on it. This is the opportunity for such players to secure recognition, and the coach should develop this as much as possible. He needs these players, and should see that they get deserved recognition.

It takes a smarter player to play defense. The offensive player knows his move. The defensive player must react to and anticipate the offensive opponent's moves. He must be real tough and rugged to stay with the offensive player. The good solid player will accept the defensive challenge. The coach must take the ability he has in his players and develop a defensive attitude that will promote a hard-nosed approach to stopping the opponents.

There is an old saying about the team having an off night in shooting or on offense, but never an off night on defense. The coach should not buy this. It is true that defense may be more consistent, because of the added factor of ball-handling skills being affected by pressures more quickly, but teams can and do have off nights on defense. Such off nights can be due to poor preparation or to psychological factors, but they do happen. The coach can point these facts out. Also, it should be pointed out that many of the off nights on the offense are brought about by the added pressure of an excellent defense. Most of the time this is the real reason for the off night that the offense has.

The cliché that "a good offensive man can beat a good defensive man any time or every time" is not to be accepted as the truth, or as a fact. The offensive player may beat the defensive player lots of times, or most of the time, but the defensive player must be coached to play the percentages. If the defensive player can put on an extra added effort from time to time, and stop the offensive player once, twice, or three or more times in a row, he may provide the offensive slow-down for the opponents needed to give the margin of victory. The team should be coached so that teammates are always alert to help the defensive man guarding the opponent with the ball. All should focus on him. He is the only one that can score.

A coach does not always have the advantage of scouting reports on his opponents, but when he does, he should exploit the report in every way possible to prepare his team for their defensive play against the opponents. It can be a tremendous psychological weapon. Handled properly, a scouting report can be worth many points.

Any time the coach is working on defense, he should also remember that he is working on offense. It takes an offense to oppose the defense. Likewise, when working on offense, the coach should remember that it takes a defense doing its best to make the offense effective and powerful. When working on the multiple and changing defensive system advocated in these pages, the coach must know that using several defenses and rotating them helps prepare the offense to meet the variations in defense that it will meet during a game and during the course of the season.

Through constant effort, emphasis, motivation, and work on defense, the coach can build a great team unity that will carry over into every phase of the game, giving the much-sought-after championships.

The coach must remember that the unheralded defensive players are the real scorers in the game.

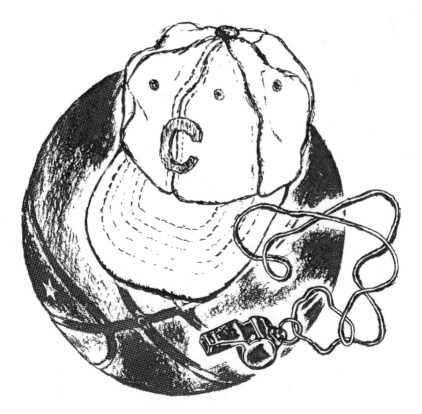

Index